Make th

BKB Verlag

VISIT THE CITY

BONN
AT A GLANCE

3 Days in

City Walk · Bonn by Night · Government Quarter · Haus der Geschichte · Strolling and Shopping · Bonn & Its Surroundings from the River · Kunstmuseum

Contents

LEGEND

- ☒ Length of walk
- ◆ Opening times/ departure times
- ▲ Transport stop
- ➤ see

Editor:
Dr. Brigitte Hintzen-Bohlen

Layout:
Andreas Ossig
BKB Verlags GmbH

Translation into English:
John Sykes, Cologne

Printing:
Brandt GmbH, Bonn

ISBN 978-3-940914-58-3

All contents and information
have been conscientiously
researched and carefully che-
cked. Nevertheless it is not
always possible to avoid errors
entirely. We are therefore
pleased to receive corrections
and proposals for additions.

BKB Verlags GmbH
Auerstrasse 4
50733 Köln
Telephone 0221/9521460
Fax   0221/5626446
www.bkb-verlag.de
mail@bkb-verlag.de

Welcome to ...

... the Federal City of Bonn, where Beethoven was born and the Federal Republic of Germany began its existence. Founded as a Roman military camp, in the Middle Ages Bonn was significant thanks to its location on an important European trade route. Later prince electors resided there, and the city was the political heart of the Federal Republic for 50 years. Today Bonn is the German base of the United Nations and an important centre for science.

Romans, archbishops, merchants and parliamentarians have all left their traces here, and made their unmistakable mark on Bonn over a period of more than 2000 years: the ruins of the Godesburg castle, the 1500-year-old minster, the Romanesque double church in Schwarzrheindorf, palaces of the prince electors, half-timbered

houses, fine residences from the late 19th century, and not least the buildings of the former government quarter, are impressive witnesses to the past. One great attraction is the Museum Mile, site of a number of important museums such as the Haus der Geschichte (House of History), the Museum König and the Bundeskunsthalle (Federal Art Gallery), which is known for its outstanding changing exhibitions. Beyond these, the Beethoven-Haus and the Macke-Haus, the Deutsches Museum and the Arithmeum are further highlights that are worth a visit.

In addition to Bonn's many sights, numerous events attract visitors to the city: its most famous resident is honoured at the annual Beethovenfest, a four-week music festival. The Internationale Stummfilmtage (Silent Film Festival) and the Prix Pantheon are well-known. The fair Pützchens Markt, the Rhein in Flammen light spectacle and Bonn's Carnival are occasions for big celebrations.

The zest for life of the Rhinelanders can be felt on all sides in this vibrant university town. Around the market square, but also in many spots in the attractive Südstadt district, in Poppelsdorf and in the Nordstadt, cafés, bars and restaurants are inviting places to linger. Those who would like some exercise will appreciate the Rheinaue, a landscaped park by the Rhine, and the surroundings of the city: Bonn's situation on both banks of the river make it the gateway to the romantic Rhine.

About Bonn

● Bonn's status as a FEDERAL CITY makes it a political location: six of the 15 federal ministries are based here and 20 federal organisations, including the Bundeskartellamt (Cartel Office) and the Bundesrechnungshof (Audit Office), as well as 29 diplomatic missions and representations.

● Bonn is a CENTRE OF INTERNATIONAL COOPERATION. Many international and internationally active institutions and organisations, including 17 bodies that are part of the United Nations and the secretariat of the UN Framework Convention on Climate Change, are established here.

● Not just since the completion of the World Conference Center Bonn, the city hosts major conferences that make it a leading PLACE FOR CONGRESSES. Such important events as two World Climate Change Summits, the Water Conference, the Afghanistan Conferences, the Renewable Energy Conference and in 2008 the UN Conference on Biological Diversity have taken place here.

● With its university, six other higher education institutions, five Fraunhofer Institutes and three Max Planck Institutes, the German Aeronautics and Space Centre (DLR), the caesar research centre, the Alanus school and a number of other leading German agencies for disseminating and promoting scientific research, Bonn has gained an international reputation as a CENTRE OF SCIENCE.

● As the birthplace of Ludwig van Beethoven, Bonn honours its famous composer. BEETHOVEN'S TOWN is home to the Beethoven-Haus, a museum and research centre, as well as the Beethoven Orchestra,

based in the Beethoven-Halle, which advertises Bonn as a city of music with concerts in Germany and abroad. At the annual Beethovenfest, world-famous musicians and up-and-coming talent perform in Bonn.

● The round nib for fountain pens and the "round writing" style, the model for today's style of HANDWRITING, was invented in Bonn by Friedrich Soennecken, a businessman who moved his company to the district of Poppelsdorf in 1876 and also produced files for documents there.

● In the Botanical Garden of the university you can admire the world's largest flower, the TITAN ARUM, which even made it into the Guinness Book of Records in 2003.

● On the 5946-metre-long PLANET TRAIL along the Rhine a proportional model of the solar system is represented on a scale of 1:1 billion.

● CARNIVAL is celebrated exuberantly in Bonn under the rule of the Carnival Prince and his princess, Bonna. The washerwomen of Beuel storm Beuel town hall on Weiberfastnacht (women's day) to set the festivities

rolling. The highlights are the camp of the city guards on Carnival Sunday and the procession through the city centre on the Monday.

● The first Bonner known by name was PUBLIUS CLODIUS, a Roman legionary, who came from Gaul in AD 35. His tombstone with a Latin inscription can be seen in the Rheinisches Landesmuseum.

● Bonn University is over 200 years old. It has brought many RESEARCHERS and SCHOLARS to the city, including the writer Ernst Moritz Arndt, the philosopher August Wilhelm von Schlegel, the physicist Heinrich Hertz, Josef Ratzinger (Pope Benedict XVI), and two Nobel Prize-winners, the physicist Wolfgang Paul and the economist Reinhard Selten.

● The Finkenberg, a small hill in the district of Limperich, is the most northerly VINEYARD in the Rhineland.

1. Münsterplatz
2. Münster
3. Sterntor
4. Zum Gequetschten
5. Beethoven-Haus
6. Market Place
7. Old Town Hall
8. St. Remigius
9. Friedrich-Wilhelms-University
10. Akademisches Kunstmuseum
11. Alter Zoll

- Café Fassbender
- Varie Tee
- Biergarten Alter Zoll
- Kessel's Espresso Studio

Day 1

City Walk

City Walk

Bonn by Night

Government Quarter

Haus der Geschichte

Strolling and Shopping

Bonn & Its Surroundings from the River

Kunstmuseum

3 Days In

CASSIUS AND FLORENTIUS

A window and two 18th-century wooden busts with golden cloaks in the minster, heads sculpted from granite on Münsterplatz – Cassius and Florentius are everywhere in the city. According to a legend they were soldiers of the Theban Legion who died the death of martyrs and were buried in the Roman cemetery where the minster

now stands. Saint Helena, the mother of Emperor Constantine the Great, is said to have built a first church in their honour: the "basilica ss. Cassii et Florentii", as it is called in the earliest written record, dating from 691–692.

In 1166 the two martyrs were proclaimed as saints, when their bones were taken from their tomb under Archbishop Reinald von Dassel. Since 1244 they have adorned the municipal seal of Bonn, and since 1643 they have been revered as the patron saints of the city.

MUSICIANS AND PRINCE ELECTORS A CITY WALK

On a stroll through the city centre you will get to know two Roman soldiers, learn little-known facts about Bonn's most famous son, and meet students in the palace of the prince electors.

● MÜNSTERPLATZ: This walk through the centre starts at Münsterplatz, the square next to the minster, site of a monument to Ludwig van Beethoven. Its inauguration ceremony in 1845 was witnessed by King Friedrich Wilhelm IV of Prussia and Queen Victoria of England from the balcony of the house on the west side of the square. The late Baroque Palais Fürstenberg houses the main post office today.

In the Middle Ages, courts of law were

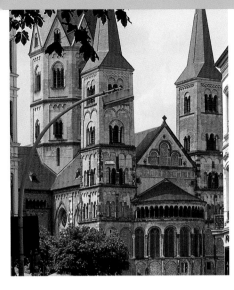

held on Münsterplatz. This is commemorated by a 2.70-metre-high Roman sandstone column in front of the main entrance. A ball made from trachyte stone, symbolising the globe and representing the ruler's power to dispense justice, tops the column. A broken-off iron plug halfway up shows that sentenced criminals were chained to the column, which

served as a pillory where bystanders mocked them.

● MÜNSTER: With the tall spire over its crossing, topping one of its five towers, the minster dominates the city skyline and is Bonn's landmark, and has been part of the city seal since the 13th century. The church is dedicated to Saints Cassius and Florentius, two Roman soldiers who died during persecutions of Christians in the 3rd century. A small, late Roman building, constructed in their honour over the tomb, evolved by the year 1248, the date when the foundation stone of the cathedral in nearby Cologne was laid, into a cross-shaped basilica, one of the finest and largest churches in the Rhineland.

KLAIS ORGANS ...

... are highly valued on every continent. In the cathedrals of Aachen and Cologne, the Megaron in Kuala Lumpur, the Philharmonic Hall of St Petersburg and the National Theatre in Beijing – organs made by the company Johannes Klais Orgelbau GmbH & Co. KG are played all over the world. Founded in 1882 by Johannes Klais and now managed by his fourth-generation descendants, the production site is still situated in Kölnstrasse in Bonn. In addition to making

new organs, Klais restore old instruments such as the globally unique organ consisting of 832 bamboo pipes in Las Piñas in the Philippines, which was built in 1824 by the Spanish priest Diego Cerra, dismantled in 1975 for its parts to be transported to Bonn, and restored there in the appropriate climatic conditions.

www.klais.de

ZUM GEQUETSCHTEN

At this Rhenish inn, a real Bonn institution that goes back over 400 years, the menu revolves around regional favourites such as "heaven and earth", pork knuckle with sauerkraut and "half a chicken" (see page 52). Its unusual name, meaning "squashed", derives from the days when country people came into town in processions behind a leader carrying a cross, and took refreshments in this lively inn by the city gate. As they could not take their saviour to the bar with them, the crucifix was carefully placed behind the door, but as the inn filled up, got squeezed in more and more between the door and the wall. As word of this spread, the inn gained its name.

Sternstrasse 78
◆ Mon-Sat
10.30am-1am,
Sun 12 noon-10pm
www.bredderbud.de

The papal coat of arms above the main entrance to the church refers to its elevation to the status of a "basilica minor": its history, beauty and great size made it the "most valuable" monument in the city, according to Pope Pius XII's proclamation of this honour in 1956.

After looking around the church nave and taking in the crypt, the final place of rest for the two patron saints of Bonn, and the imposing Klais organ, continue through the heavy metal door on the south side of the nave.

It leads to one of the most beautiful spots in Bonn, listed as one of the "1000 places to see before you die": the Romanesque cloister. This wonderful haven of peace was built in the mid-12th century by the dean, Gerhard von der Aue, along with the two-storey collegiate building.

On the three surviving wings of the cloister, note the elaborately decorated capitals with flower-like decoration.

Münsterplatz
◆ Mon-Sat
7.30am-6.45pm,
Sun 8.30am-7.15pm
www.bonner-muenster.de

● STERNTOR: Next, walk along Vivatsgasse to the "Star Gate",

THE OLD CEMETERY

The Alter Friedhof, a cemetery laid out in 1715, originally only for "common inhabitants, passers-by and soldiers" outside the town walls, is a place to stroll through Bonn's cultural and intellectual history. Remodelled as a jardin parlant ("talking garden") in the 19th century, it is a lovely peaceful spot today. Great old trees shade the graves of many leading persons from the fields of art, science and politics, including Ernst Moritz Arndt, August Wilhelm von Schlegel, the brothers Boisserée, Robert Schumann and Mildred Scheel, and the works of famous sculptors such as Schinkel, Rauch, Stüler and Donndorf.

Sterntor, a reminder of the medieval town fortifications that once existed here. To allow the traffic to flow better, in 1898 the gate at the end of Sternstrasse, the entrance to Bonn for goods

coming from Aachen, was demolished and this replacement gate was constructed only a few metres away using remnants of the old town wall. Two sculptures are visible on the gate: a late Gothic group of the crucified Christ with Mary and St John, and the Virgin of the Seven Sorrows, dating from 1650.

Bornheimer Strasse 77
▲ *Heerstrasse*
◆ *7am-8pm (summer), 8am-5pm (winter), Tours: Sat 11am, Sun 2pm (May-Oct)*
www.alter-friedhof-bonn.de

Have a Break

Café Fassbender in the pedestrian zone is a good stop-off for cakes and other culinary treats.

Sternstrasse 55, ◆ *Mon-Sat 9.30am-7pm, Sun 11.30am-6pm*

BEETHOVENFEST

The music festival that is held in Bonn for one month each autumn in honour of the greatest native of the town originated in the three-day celebration held in 1845, when the monument to Beethoven on Münsterplatz was inaugurated. Attention focusses not only on Beethoven's music, but also on how it is received in modern times. Top international orchestras, leading ensembles, prominent soloists and promising young musicians present programmes that they have devised especially for this festival. In addition newly commissioned works are premiered, and creative young media artists present their take on Beethoven in short films, installations and video clips.

www. beethoven fest.de

● BEETHOVEN-HAUS: The *5th Symphony*, the *Moonlight Sonata*, *For Elise* and the opera *Fidelio* – just a few of many famous works by the composer Ludwig van Beethoven, who was born in December 1770 in the garden wing of the house at Bonngasse 20. When twelve enthusiastic citizens of Bonn founded the Beethoven-Haus Association in 1889, the house where the composer was born in Bonngasse became a place of memorial that documents the composer's life and work in what is now the world's largest Beethoven collection.

Here you can find out how the young Beethoven lived, following the stages of a career that took him to the Viennese Classical style and made him a forerunner of Romantic music. You can learn about the people who surrounded and influenced

him, and hear the impact that his compositions made on the history of music.

Don't fail to pay a visit to the studio with digital resources in the neighbouring building, reached through the sculpture court. The studio takes you on an interactive journey of discovery though Beethoven's legacy. You can listen to his works in recordings made by the Deutsche Grammophon Gesellschaft, see a reconstruction of his last dwelling in Vienna, and listen to a reading from Beethoven's letters.

Bonngasse 18-26 (City Centre)
Tel. 0228/981750
▲ *Bertha-von-Suttner-Platz/Beethoven-Haus*
◆ *10am-6pm (April-Oct),*
Mon-Sat 10am-5pm, Sun 11am-5pm (Nov-March)
www.beethoven-haus-bonn.de

3 TIP For a completely different kind of musical experience, take a look at the project for visualising music in the historic vaulted cellar. It combines traditional and experimental means of expression, interactively presenting two selected compositions – Fidelio and Presto 126/4 – in a space with sound and 3D-graphics systems.

BEETHOVENHALLE

After the war many citizens of Bonn wished to dedicate a worthy concert hall to Beethoven once again. They raised more than one million deutschmarks, and opened the new concert and event venue on the banks of the Rhine in 1959. The Beethovenhalle, the third in Bonn to bear the name, consists of a group of irregularly shaped blocks

around a central domed structure, and is today one of the city landmarks. It is the home of the orchestra of the same name, and was the place where four federal presidents were elected in the years when Bonn was capital of Germany. For Beethoven's 250th birthday in 2020, the hall will look splendid again after a thorough refurbishment.

www.beethovenhalle.de

ST REMIGIUS

To follow in Beethoven's footsteps go a few paces further to what used to be the Franciscan church. The small bell-turret on the roof identifies it as a

church of mendicant monks. Beethoven was baptised here in the font in the left-hand aisle, and played the organ as a ten-year-old for early mass. In the course of centuries the once-precious furnishings of this early 14th-century Gothic basilica have largely been lost, leaving an interior that has a plain appearance, apart from the sculpture of the Virgin Mary on a pillar of the nave and a cycle of altar paintings by the Nazarene school.

Brüdergasse 8
◆ *8am-6pm*

● MARKETPLACE: Sternstrasse, the street of bakers in the Middle Ages (originally Pisternenstrasse from pisterna, meaning bakery) and now a popular shopping street, leads to the centre of the city, the Marktplatz. The unusual, almost triangular shape of this marketplace arose from its location at the meeting point of several old trade routes. The market fountain at the centre takes the form of a richly adorned obelisk, which the citizens erected at their own expense, on the instructions of Prince Elector Maximilian Friedrich, following a great fire in 1777.

To make the most of these splendid historic surroundings, stroll between the vegetable stalls on the market before taking a seat at one of the many cafés. Many historic buildings can be seen here, including Bonn's oldest inn, Em Höttche, where Elisabeth Kurzrock ("Shortskirt") is said to have been burned as a witch in 1628 and the young Beethoven danced with his sweetheart

Have a Break

To enjoy high-quality tea while watching the bustle on the marketplace, go to the **Varie Tee**.
Markt 6 ◆ 10am-11pm, www.varietee.de

Barbe Koch. The Metropol, now a bookshop, was the last large cinema in the Art Deco style.

● ALTES RATHAUS: Both an eye-catcher and an emblem of the city, the Old Town Hall with its opulent Rococo façade stands on the broad east side of the marketplace. Prince Elector Clemens August personally laid its foundation stone in 1737 – the two golden lions, the electors' heraldic animals, on the mansard roof are a reference to this. Be sure to walk up the double-flight steps with their gilded railings, which have been the scene of historic events. The first president of the Federal Republic of Germany, Theodor Heuss, addressed the citizens from here in 1949. Speeches were made here in 1962 by Charles de Gaulle and a year later by John F. Kennedy, and the Soviet head of state Mikhail Gorbachev was greeted with cheers on this spot.

THE CITY COAT OF ARMS

Take a look inside the vestibule of the Altes Rathaus to see a cast of the "little stone wolf", as a Roman sculpture of a lion killing a wild boar is called locally. Until the end of the prince electors' rule it stood on Münsterplatz, next to the pillory (➤ p. 11), where the courts of law sat. The lion as a symbol of the judiciary stands on the lower part of Bonn's coat of arms, while the upper part is the black cross on a silver ground of Electoral Cologne, to show the connection between Bonn and the prince electors of Cologne.

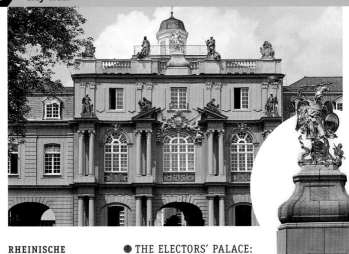

RHEINISCHE FRIEDRICH-WILHELMS-UNIVERSITÄT

Traditional and modern – that is not a contradiction in Bonn. Top-level research that gains world-

wide recognition and historic surroundings are today the hallmarks of Bonn's university, the Rheinische Friedrich-Wilhelms-Universität, named after King Friedrich Wilhelm III of Prussia, who founded it in 1818. With some 35,000 students and a wide range of faculties, from Asian studies to dentistry, this is one of the largest universities in Germany. The international character of its research makes it a highly respected scientific institution at home and abroad.

www.uni-bonn.de

● THE ELECTORS' PALACE:

The next stop is the Kurfürstliches Schloss, for centuries a residence of the Prince Electors of Cologne and today the main building of the university. This castle-like complex of four wings, crowned by towers and enclosing several courtyards, was built between 1697 and 1705 by Enrico Zuccali, the court architect in Munich. Almost 20 years later it was extended to the south and the Baroque Hofgarten was laid out – a park that made history when Bonn was the federal capital, and many anti-government demonstrations were held here. Today its location makes it a popular park among the students.

Above the gateway to the Hofgarten, the golden statue of Regina Pacis, the Queen of Peace and patron of the university, keeps watch. She has proven qualities of endurance, having survived the five-day fire of 1777, the French occupation and the heavy bombing raid of 1944.

Note the Baroque triumphal gate by the Bonn architect Michel Leveilly, which spans Adenauerallee. Its true name is St Michael's Gate, because this part of the building originally served as the seat of the Order of Knights of Saint Michael. This is why it is topped by a bronze statue of the archangel Michael waving his sword at the snaking coils of the dragon (the original is on the first floor of the palace). However, the popular name for the gate, which lies above road B9 to Koblenz, is simply Koblenzer Tor.

● AKADEMISCHES KUNSTMUSEUM: While at the university, it is worth taking a detour to what was once the anatomy building at the end of the Hofgarten. This beautiful Neoclassical rotunda, a work by Schinkel, catches the eye from a distance. It is home to Bonn's oldest museum, the university's collection of antiquities, and takes visitors on a journey through the art of the ancient world. Since 1819, when Friedrich Gottlieb Welcker became professor of classical archaeology and head of the collection of antiquities, Greek and Roman works of art from the Mediterranean region have been gathered here, in the form of originals and casts.

POPPELSDORFER SCHLOSS

A visit to the 18th-century Baroque palace that now belongs to the university and holds its collections on natural science is worthwhile even in bad weather. This complex of four wings, whose arcaded courtyard is the setting in summer for the Poppelsdorfer Schlosskonzerte, concerts of classical music, forms a visual axis with the church on the Kreuzberg and the electors' palace, to which a wide avenue of chestnut trees connects it. Don't miss a stroll through what used to be the palace garden and is now the Botanical Garden, one of the oldest and most species-rich in the world, and famous for the spectacular flowering of its gigantic titan arum.

Botanischer Garten, Meckenheimer Allee 171
◆ Sun-Wed, Fri 10am-6pm, Thu 10am-8pm (April-Oct),
Mon-Fri 10am-4pm (Nov-March)
www.botgart.uni-bonn.de

FIGURE ON THE BRIDGE

If you walk along the Rhine promenade to

Kennedybrücke, you will see a stone figure showing its backside. Because Beuel across the river made no contribution to the cost of building the first bridge over the Rhine in 1898, the people of Bonn added this cheeky figure, which then showed its backside to Beuel. The answer from the other side was a scolding washerwoman. Since post-war restoration of the bridge, the figure has pointed south to Frankfurt, which had just been defeated by Bonn in its bid to be capital city.

With its ancient ceramics, statuettes, bronze and terracotta works and many casts of well-known masterpieces such as the tyrant-slayers from the Parthenon frieze, the Hermes of Olympia and Laocoon, this museum is a veritable treasure house for lovers of classical antiquity.

Am Hofgarten 21, ◆ Tue-Fri 3-5pm, Sun 11am-6pm www.antikensammlung.uni-bonn.de

● ALTER ZOLL: The last stop on this city stroll is the old customs station for collecting tolls from Rhine trade, which stood on a bastion at the corner of

Bonn's city walls. Today this terrace with its shady chestnut trees and a bronze monument to the poet Ernst-Moritz Arndt is worth visiting for a wonderful view over the Rhine to the Siebengebirge hills. The temple gateway at the foot of the Alter Zoll is a work of homage to Heinrich Heine by the artist Ulrich Rückriem.

Have a Break

Drink a glass of Kölsch in the adjacent **Alter Zoll** beer garden with a splendid view of the Rhine.

Am Brassertufer ◆ 11am-midnight (summer)

Bonn by Night

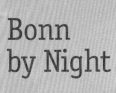

THE RHINE IN FLAMES

On the first Saturday in May each year, hundreds of thousands of people flock to the Rhine to see the riverbank and the sights between Linz and Bonn bathed in festive light by glowing red torches. Spectators on the bridges and banks can watch a fleet of 60 illuminated ships sailing up and down this stretch of river, accompanied by five sets of firework. The finale is a musical display of fireworks high in the air above the Rheinaue park, where a fair with a free programme of entertainment takes place at the same time.

www.rhein-in-flammen-bonn.de

CULTURE OR DANCING – BONN BY NIGHT

Those who think that Bonn has nothing to offer in terms of nightlife are wrong. In addition to cultural events, there are lots of pubs, and party people can celebrate into the early hours!

If you are looking forward to a cultural evening, Bonn has a wide range of offerings. With opera, concerts by the Beethoven-Orchester and the Klassische Philharmonie, as well as jazz, rock and pop concerts, Bonn lives up to its name as a city of music. Its theatre scene too has much to offer – alongside the municipal ensemble there are many privately run theatres and cabarets, such as the well-known Pantheon and the Haus der Springmaus. The latter is situated in the Kultur-meile ("cultural mile") of Frongasse in Endenich, where the Harmonie music club, Fiddler's Irish Pub for Irish folk music, the Rex cinema, the Robert-Schumann-Haus and the Theater im Ball-saal are to be found.

LINDENWIRTIN ÄNNCHEN ...

... must be one of the best-known Bad Godesberg personalities. She was given the freedom of Bonn, and even received congratulations from the former Emperor Wilhelm II on her 75th birthday. Ännchen Schumacher (1860–1935) wanted to be a teacher, but had to take over her parents' inn at the age of 18 after her father's death. Her jolly Rhineland mentality, lovable way of exercising authority and uncommon musical talent soon made the inn popular. More than 500 students from a great variety of student corps are said to have drunk together harmoniously every

If you prefer dancing, there are various places around the city centre, and for a few drinks, the options in and near the pedestrian zone range from traditional Rhineland pubs serving Kölsch beer from Cologne, such as Bönnsch at the Sterntorbrücke, which brews its own beer, to a Bavarian beer hall, the Irish pub and a number of cocktail bars. In a city where many students live there is no shortage of places to go out, and party-goers find something to meet their taste in such locations as Blow Up, 3-Raum-Wohnung and Panorama.

For a leisurely pub crawl try the Südstadt, a middle-class district south of the Hofgarten and Poppelsdorfer Allee where many pubs and cafés thrive.

summer evening, a state of affairs that was known as the "peace of Bad Godesberg". She gained her nickname "Lindenwirtin" (landlady of the Linde) from a well-known student song.

The inn is closed at present.

BEUEL

On the opposite side of the Rhine lies the district of Beuel, which means "high ground" in Middle High German. Beuel, now part of Bonn, has been widely known since the mid-18th century. A place where many laundries operated, it was the cradle of the Rhineland custom of Weiberfastnacht, the women's day in Carnival. In order to celebrate the most important day of Carnival, which was then male-dominated, in 1824 several emancipated washerwomen formed the Alte Beueler Damenkomitee. To this day this society's "laundry princess" and her committee of women still symbolically take over the town hall of Beuel after a big Weiberfastnacht parade.

With its beautiful houses dating from the late 19th and early 20th century and small front gardens, the Südstadt is also an architectural gem, one of the largest coherent ensembles in Germany to be preserved from the period between 1865 and 1918. Walk a little further to Poppelsdorf, where you will find a lively pub scene behind the Botanical Garden along Clemens-August-Strasse.

Less mainstream is the nightlife in the inner Nordstadt (also called Altstadt), a 100-year-old middle-class and artisan quarter to the north of the city centre. There are many pubs and restaurants in this multicultural district with a Mediterranean

atmosphere around Breite Strasse and Heerstrasse. Don't fail to take a look into the pretty back yards, where a buzzing art scene has moved into artisans' workshops and factories.

Listings: www.bonnaparte.de

Government Quarter

BONN – CAPITAL OF THE FEDERAL REPUBLIC

In 1949, during the search for a provisional capital of the Federal Republic, Bonn seemed ideal. This quiet little town had not been severely damaged in the war, had no military and industrial past, provided enough space for offices and housing, and had an airport nearby. Moreover, in contrast to Frankfurt,

its closest rival, Bonn was not a threat to Berlin, the city that was named as capital in the constitution. The residence of Chancellor Konrad Adenauer in Rhöndorf was very close to Bonn, but how far this fact played a role can no longer be ascertained. Bonn became a capital city with ambitions, and in 1973 the word "provisional" was deleted. Nevertheless, those who favoured Berlin were to have their way, as Bonn could not compete with Berlin after German reunification in 1990.

THE DEMOCRACY TRAIL – GOVERNMENT QUARTER

The programme for this walk is not only politics. First you will learn about the diversity of species on earth, then follow the history of the Federal Republic, and finally visit some buildings of the "provisional" German capital.

● MUSEUM KOENIG ❶: This imposing sandstone building is home to the natural history museum that the zoologist Alexander König founded and handed over to the city of Bonn in 1929. The permanent exhibition Our Blue Planet – Life in the Network is equally fascinating for adults and children. It gives an entertaining explanation of ecological dependencies within and between the most

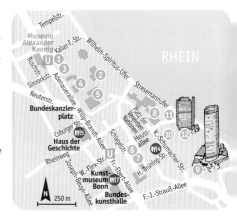

important ecosystems of the earth. From the African savannah to tropical rainforest, the desert and the Antarctic, here you can experience nature with all your senses. The dioramas from the time when the museum was founded are a highlight. These protected heritage items have been restored and integrated into the exhibition.

At the same time the museum is the starting point of the Democracy Trail, which leads through the 50-year history of the government quarter and points out the former or current political importance of the buildings there on information boards. After the end of the war, the museum courtyard was the site of a historic event: on 1 September 1948 the Parliamentary Council which wrote the German constitution was established here.

Adenauerallee 160 (Museumsmeile)
Tel. 0228/91220
▲ *Museum Koenig*
◆ *Tue, Thu-Sun 10am-6pm, Wed 10am-9pm*
www.museumkoenig.de

3 TIP If you want to see Adenauer's desk or stand on the terrace of Villa Hammerschmidt, home of the president of the Federal Republic, plan your walk in advance, as many buildings in the government quarter are only open to the public as part of a guided tour.

Information: Bonn-Information,
tel. 0172/7718978, and www.bonntouren.de

THE BONN-BERLIN LAW

When members of parliament decided in favour of Berlin as the new seat of government and parliament after a passionate all-day debate on 20 June 1991, with a narrow majority of 338 to 320 votes, of course there had to be compensation for Bonn. On 7 May 1994 a law therefore stipulated that nine federal ministries would move to Berlin, while six would remain in Bonn. Demands for a complete move of all ministries to Berlin, although regularly repeated, have always met with rejection. 20 years on, the results of the capital-city changes seem to be favourable for Bonn, as it is now the seat of many international organisations and an outstanding centre for scientific research.

THE CHANCELLOR'S BUNGALOW ❷

Ludwig Erhard, for whom it was built, wanted his residence to symbolise openness and democracy, and also to be a place for meetings and dialogue. In the park of Palais Schaumburg the architect

Sep Ruf thus created a low building with glass walls and panorama windows down to floor level. It is considered an outstanding example of West German post-war architecture. Not all subsequent chancellors praised it as much as Erhard, but they received kings and presidents here until the federal government moved to Berlin.

*Adenauerallee 139
(Museumsmeile)
Visits only as part of a
guided tour (via the
Haus der Geschichte,
tel. 0228/9165400)*

● VILLA HAMMERSCHMIDT ❸: Diagonally opposite, in a five-hectare landscaped park, lies the late Neoclassical house that has been the residence and office of the German president since 1950 and is sometimes described as "Bonn's White House". When Richard von Weizsäcker moved his official seat to Schloss Bellevue in Berlin in 1994, Villa Hammerschmidt took second place. It is named after the industrialist Rudolf Hammerschmidt, who bought the magnificent house dating from the mid-19th century from Leopold König, the father of the famous zoologist, in 1899.

*Adenauerallee 135 (Museumsmeile)
Visits only as part of a guided tour*

● PALAIS SCHAUMBURG ❹: A little further along, this splendid late Neoclassical residence with a graceful round tower has also seen many historic events. For a time it was the centre of Bonn society, when

Wilhelmine Viktoria of Prussia, daughter of the German emperor, moved in with her husband Prince Adolf Wilhelm Victor von Schaumburg-Lippe in 1891. After the founding of the Federal Republic of Germany, the palais became the chancellor's office. By 1976 the premises had become inadequate, and a new chancellery was built. Since 1999 Palais Schaumburg has been the second seat of the chancellery and federal chancellor.

Adenauerallee 139-141 (Museumsmeile)
Visits only as part of a guided tour (via the Haus der Geschichte, tel. 0228/9165400)

● BUNDESKANZLERAMT ❺: As Palais Schaumburg no longer met the technical and spatial requirements of government operations, in 1973 a new chancellery was built. This plain, low building with every technical refinement, which Helmut Schmidt described as having the "charm of a savings bank", is now the headquarter of the Federal Ministry of Economic Cooperation and Development. The golden sculpture that Helmut Schmidt had placed in front of the building, *Two Large Forms* by Henry Moore, is world-famous. A monument to Konrad Adenauer represents the Bonn years of the Federal Republic: various symbols on the back of Adenauer's head present stages in the life of the first chancellor.

Adenauerallee 141 (Museumsmeile)
Visits only as part of a guided tour

THE TULIP FIELD ❻

The Tulpenfeld (Tulip Field), an office complex built in the 1960s on land that had been used for farming, became famous for the government press conferences that were held here from 1968. The Bundespressekonferenz, an association of parliamentary correspondents that was founded in 1949 as an institution independent of the government, holds press conferences with prominent persons from the fields of politics, business and the arts, including government press conferences three times weekly at fixed times. Until 4 August 1999 they took place in the meeting room of the Pressehaus with its two long glass walls, which is today an outstation. The other occupants of the complex are the Bundesnetzagentur and development organisations.

DEUTSCHE WELLE ❼

The Schürmannbau, a building at the foot of the two skyscrapers Langer Eugen and Post-Tower, was originally built as an extension of the building that accommodates members of parliament. Damaged by the floods in 1993, since 2003 it has been the home of Deutsche Welle. This radio and TV station is Germany's voice in the rest of the world, broadcasting in over 30 languages via airwaves and internet. Financed entirely by the government, the aim of Deutsche Welle is to present events and trends in Germany and the world from a German point of view and thus promote understanding between different peoples and cultures.

www.dw.de

● BUNDESHAUS AND PLENARY CHAMBER ❽:

The route continues to a complex of buildings in which the Parliamentary Council was established on 1 September 1948 and passed the Grundgesetz (constitution of the Federal Republic) only eight months later on 23 May 1949. The Bundeshaus started out as a college for teachers, constructed in the Bauhaus style in the 1930s. As Bonn wanted to steal a march

on its rivals to be capital city, in 1949 the architect Hans Schwippert was commissioned to extend this building, and within a few months the first of many extensions was built: a five-storey north wing for the upper house of parliament (Bundesrat), a three-storey south wing for the lower house (Bundestag), and a plenary chamber measuring 1000 square metres.

Parliament met here for almost 40 years, until in 1986 the Bundestag decided to tear down the decaying plenary chamber and rebuild it to designs by the architect Behnisch. It was completed in 1992, a year after the decision to move the government and parliament to Berlin. Delegates were therefore able to use this prestigious building, with expanses of glass to symbolise democratic openness and transparency, for a short time only. On 1 July 1999 the

Deutscher Bundestag sat in Bonn for the last time. Today the building is part of the World Conference Center Bonn.

A new feature of the chamber was the arrangement of seating in a circle, so that members of the government and Bundesrat no longer sat opposite the delegates in a raised position, but with them in one circle. The incompleteness of the circle was symbolised by the Bundestag eagle, the so-called "fat hen", whose feathers were symmetrical but had a gap.

Platz der Nationen 8 (Museumsmeile)
Visits only as part of a guided tour

Have a Break

Ristorante Forissimo with its idyllic garden opposite Deutsche Welle invites its guests to enjoy Italian specialities.
Kurt-Schumacher-Strasse 18
◆ Mon-Fri 12 noon-2.30pm, Mon-Sat 6.30-11pm

POST-TOWER ⑨

Visible from afar, the tallest office building in North-Rhine Westphalia with a height of 162.50 meters is a symbol of the transformation of Bonn. This futuristic-looking tower of steel, glass and concrete was built for Deutsche Post DHL in 2002 by the architects Jahn and Murphy. Its ground plan consists of a three-storey base and two

slightly displaced elliptical halves, joined together by delicate structures of steel and glass on every ninth floor by a so-called sky garden, a transparent glass surface. After dark the tower makes its mark on the night sky in Bonn thanks to a dynamic light installation by the Breton artist Yann Kersalé.

Platz der
Deutschen Post,
visits only as part of a
guided tour (information
from Bonn-Information)
and on open day.

UN CAMPUS ⑩

When many United Nations organisations were established in Bonn in the 1990s, the German government decided to bring together in one location those bodies that worked principally in the field of the environment and sustainability. The renovation of former parliament buildings since 2006 has created the so-called UN Campus, which has been placed permanently at the disposal of the UN and is now home to 20 organisations, to include the United Nations Climate Change Secretariat.

www.un.org

● WASSERWERK ⑪: 364 sessions of the Bundestag were held here, including the historic meeting on 20 June 1991 that took the decision to move the parliament and government to Berlin. Those who enter the Wasserwerk, which used to be the pump house of a waterworks built in 1892 and today is part of the World Conference Center Bonn, are surprised at how small it is. However, while the new plenary chamber was being constructed, the location of this waterworks made it extremely suitable as alternative accommodation. Members of parliament were willing to live with the cramped seating, even when space had to be found for 144 new members from the former East Germany after reunification in 1990.

Platz der Nationen 2 (Museumsmeile)
Visits only as part of a guided tour

● LANGER EUGEN ⑫: Directly opposite stands the building that was formerly used for members of the Deutscher Bundestag, erected in 1969 to designs by the architect Egon Eiermann and for many years the tallest building in Bonn at 114.70 metres. Its nickname is Langer Eugen (Tall Eugen), a joking reference to the small stature of Eugen Gerstenmeyer, the president of the Bundestag who worked hard to get the 29-storey tower built. Today it is the centre of the UN Campus, as three large blue-and-white illuminated emblems show from a distance.

Hermann-Ehlers-Strasse 10

Haus der Geschichte

ERNST-MORITZ-ARNDT-HAUS

From the Rhine terrace of the only professor's house from the first half of the 19th century that has survived in Bonn, you can enjoy a wonderful view of the river and the Siebengebirge hills. The house, which lay in vineyards outside the town when it was built, was the home and place of work of Ernst Moritz Arndt, a writer, professor of history and delegate to the National Assembly in Frankfurt, from 1819 until his death in 1860. Today a branch of the municipal museum, it is used for special exhibitions, and with its typical Biedermeier furnishings conveys a good impression of those days.

Adenauerallee 79
▲ *Juridicum*
◆ *Wed-Sat 1-5pm, Sun 11.30am-5pm (only during exhibitions)*
www2.bonn.de/stadtmuseum

RECONSTRUCTION AND THE ECONOMIC MIRACLE – THE HAUS DER GESCHICHTE

From the post-war period to the years of guest workers and reunification – here you can take a trip through 60 years of German political, economic and social history.

"Liberation and hope for some, defeat, disillusionment and fear for others. The unconditional surrender of the Wehrmacht on 8 May 1945 ended the Second World War, which Germany had unleashed." This is the starting point of the recent history of Germany which this unique museum brings to life on an area of more than 4000 square metres with over 7000 exhibits and 150 media points.

Hardly a single topic is left out. The post-war years can be relived with such items as registration forms for those repatriated to the French zone and a machine for cleaning up rubble. The exhibits show how two German states soon emerged from the Berlin crisis of 1948–49, and took very different courses in the following decades.

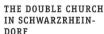

Visitors are invited to sit in a reconstruction of the chamber of the Deutscher Bundestag, as the members of parliament did from 1949 to 1987.

A Russian tank is a reference to the Cold War, which is also documented with original stones from the Berlin Wall and a secret camera in a book. The commemorative plaque that was once placed on the Deutsches Haus on the town hall square in Bremen is a reminder that the cause of German unity was never abandoned: "Remember our brothers, who bear the fate of our partition!"

Take a seat in a 1950s cinema or an ice-cream parlour with a juke box, exhibits that represent the era of the West German economic miracle in the 1950s and 1960s. The VW Beetle with window bars and running boards dating from 1950, one of the famous Vespa scooters made by the Italian company Piaggio and the double-M logo of the Leipzig trade fair are just a few items from a period when the social market economy created a new economic system combining laissez-faire and a welfare state.

THE DOUBLE CHURCH IN SCHWARZRHEIN- DORF

For lovers of medieval architecture, a trip to Schwarzrheindorf in the district of Beuel is a treat: here stands a double church dedicated to St Mary and St Clement, famous for its well-preserved Romanesque frescoes. Consecrated in 1151 by Arnold von Wied, archbishop of Cologne, it is a two-storey funerary chapel on the plan of a Greek cross, with the lower storey dedicated to St Clement and the upper storey to the Virgin Mary. An octagonal opening at the centre connects the two levels, so that the lord on his raised throne and his courtiers could follow the celebration of mass in the lower church, where the congregation worshipped.

*Dixstrasse 41
(Schwarzrheindorf)
◆ Tue–Sun 9am-6.30pm
(summer),
Tue–Sun 9am-5pm
(winter)*

SCHLOSS BRÜHL

To see a World Herit-
age site, take a trip to
Brühl, a small town near
Bonn, where a Rococo
masterpiece consisting
of Schloss Augustus-
burg, the hunting lodge
Schloss Falkenlust

and gardens has been
preserved largely in
its original condition.
Prince Elector Clemens
August von Wittelsbach,
archbishop of Cologne
(1700–1761), commis-
sioned François de Cuvil-
liés to build the palace
as his summer residence.
Many leading European
artists worked here.
Balthasar Neumann de-
signed the world-famous
stair hall, Dominique
Girard the Baroque gar-
dens in the French style.
www.schlossbruehl.de

Read how John F. Kennedy noted his famous sen-
tence "I am a Berliner" in phonetic letters on a
card in 1963, or take a look at other historical
events such as the building of the Berlin Wall,
the student protests in 1968, the first landing of
men on the moon in 1969, the award of the Nobel Peace Prize to Willy Brandt in 1971 and the
attack on the Olympic Games in 1972 in Munich,
or refresh your memory about the new Green Party in the 1970s, the fall of the Wall and German
reunification.

To follow the development of garden allotments
from the past to the present day, take a walk
through the museum garden behind the building.
On the lower floor, even more history awaits discovery in the shape of the remains of a well-preserved Roman cellar dating from the 2nd century,
probably part of a tavern in "vicus bonnensis".

Willy-Brandt-Allee 14
◆ *Tue-Fri 9am-7pm, Sat-Sun 10am-6pm*
www.hdg.de

Have a Break

Whether you choose from the "chancellor's
menu" or local dishes, the **café in the Haus
der Geschichte** is a good place to take a break
after looking at the exhibition.
Willy-Brandt-Allee 14 ◆ *Tue-Fri 11.30am-
5.30pm, Sat-Sun 11.30am-5.45pm*

Strolling and Shopping

City Walk

Bonn by Night

Government Quarter

Kunstmuseum

3
Days In

Bonn & Its Surroundings from the River

Strolling and Shopping

HOLY STEPS

For a trip close to the city centre, the place of pilgrimage on the Kreuzberg (Cross Hill) provides a wonderful view of Bonn, the Rhine and the Siebengebirge. The magnificently decorated Baroque church is a real gem, and has a copy of the Scala Santa, the steps in Rome

which are said to have come from the palace of Pontius Pilate and to have been ascended by Jesus before he was condemned. In 1746 Prince Elector Clemens August, archbishop of Cologne, commissioned the architect Balthasar Neumann to build a stair next to the choir, with relics in its middle flight of steps. It is open only on Good Friday and Easter Saturday, when pilgrims climb the 28 steps on their knees, as in Rome. On other days you can view the steps through a grille.

◆ *9am-5pm (winter),*
9am-6pm (summer)
www.kreuzberg-bonn.de

A CHARMING ATMOSPHERE

If you like to do your shopping without walking too far, and appreciate little lanes and attractive squares with street cafés and a wide selection of specialised shops and chain stores, then in Bonn you have come to the right place.

The main area for shopping in Bonn is the city centre between Münsterplatz, Marktplatz and Friedensplatz – one of Germany's largest uninterrupted pedestrian zones. The narrow streets and little lanes, which open up into squares where you can linger a while, have their own special charm. The shops cater for almost all requirements, as they range from department stores and fashion stores to a great variety of smaller shops, including specialised outlets. High-class Friedrichstrasse with its façades dating from the late 19th century and the Art Nouveau period is a particularly attractive street. Beautiful and unusual things, from furnishings to exclusive special products, are on display in the shop windows. Don't miss the lovely view from Kaiserplatz towards Schloss Poppelsdorf! In the shade of chestnut trees you can browse through the shelves of the numerous second-hand bookshops or take a break in one of the cafés.

Have a Break

In **Kessel's Espresso Studio** they serve an excellent cup of coffee.
Friedrichstrasse 54 ◆ Mon-Fri 10am-7pm, Sat 10am-6pm

Bonn & Its Surroundings
from the River

GODESBURG

Visible from afar, the 39-metre-high keep of ruined castle in Bad Godesberg rises above the district of the same name. One of the first hill-top castles on the Rhine, it was built in 1210 by Archbishop Dietrich I and for many decades was a favourite residence of the archbishops of Cologne, until it was blown up in 1583 during the Seneschal's War. Its charm was rediscovered in the Romantic era, and today the Godesburg has been converted into a restaurant. From the tower, a wonderful 360-degree panorama of the Rhine valley reaches as far as the Cologne area and the Siebengebirge.

Tower: Auf dem Godesberg 5
◆ Wed-Sun 10am-6pm
(April-Oct)

THE GATEWAY TO THE ROMANTIC RHINE – BONN & ITS SURROUNDINGS FROM THE RIVER

For the fabled Siebengebirge hills and Drachenfels, the Roland Arch, the piers of the famous bridge in Remagen and the half-timbered town of Linz, a trip on the Rhine is an essential part of a visit to Bonn.

Bonn, where 200 years ago artists and intellectuals set off on study trips, and inspired many others to visit the romantic Rhine with their enthusiastic writings, poems and works of art, is the gateway to one of the loveliest stretches of the river. Don't miss the opportunity to take an excursion past the Siebengebirge to Linz, passing picturesque little towns, fine residences and sites of great natural beauty. You can leave the boat at any stop and spend time in a spot that takes your fancy.

The trip begins at the **Alter Zoll** pier, from where the boats go south towards the government quarter, giving you a view of the garden of Villa Hammerschmidt. Beyond the Konrad Adenauer Bridge, on the right bank shortly before you reach the landing stage in Oberkassel, lie the Kameha Grand Hotel (➤ p. 51) and Rohmühle (➤ p. 55). You pass the castle-like Haus Carstanjen, home of the Federal Treasury Ministry until it

was abolished in 1969. Today the building is used by the UN. Next come Niederdollendorf and **Bad Godesberg**, where splendid houses built in the late 19th century and residences on the Rhine might tempt you to take a stroll through the diplomatic history of this district of Bonn.

Opposite the historic Rheinhotel Dreesen, where luminaries such as Greta Garbo and Marlene once stayed, extends the hilly area known as the Siebengebirge. You will see the Petersberg and its hotel, formerly the government guest house (➤ p. 50), and the Drachenfels, a peak with a ruined castle that is famed in legend.

REDOUTE

In the spa Bad Godesberg, whose mineral springs were known back in Roman times, the Redoutenpark, six and a half hectares landscaped in the

English style, is a pleasant place for a walk. Between 1790 and 1792 Prince Elector Max Franz of Bavaria built a Neoclassical ballroom here, where court society amused itself at masked balls. The building with three wings, where the young Beethoven played in front of Joseph Haydn in 1792 and the world premiere of *The Magic Flute* took place in 1793, was later a casino, a clubhouse and a place for state receptions during the French occupation. Today the Redoute hosts various events, and the adjacent gardener's house, the Redüttchen, is home to a restaurant (➤ p. 53).

SIEBENGEBIRGE

It is not known whether the "seven hills" take their name from seven giants, who according to a legend were making access to the Rhine for a town, and after finishing work created the hills by cleaning their dirty spades; or whether the word "Siefen", meaning the wet valleys of streams, gave the name to these volcanic hills. Either way, this area on the right bank of the Rhine to the south-east of Bonn, with its 42 hills, is Germany's oldest nature reserve. More than 200 kilometres of walking trails criss-cross this forested area.

www.siebengebirge.com

To see more of the Siebengebirge, get off the boat at **Königswinter**, where a rack-and-pinion railway takes you up the hill to where Siegfried is said to have slain the dragon and to a neo-Gothic palace, Schloss Drachenburg. As an alternative, visit the Siebengebirgsmuseum in this little wine town or admire native species of the underwater world at Sealife.

Schloss Drachenburg:
◆ *11am-6pm (April-Oct), www.drachenfels.net*

Siebengebirgsmuseum:
Kellerstrasse 16, ◆ Tue-Fri 2-5pm, Sat 2-6pm, Sun 11am-6pm, www.siebengebirgsmuseum.de

Sealife:
Rheinallee 8, ◆ 10am-5pm(Oct-March), 10am-6pm (April-Sept), www.visitsealife.com

The next stop is **Bad Honnef** opposite Nonnenwerth island, known as Nice-on-the-Rhine on account of its mild climate. Here you can walk into the town centre from the boat jetty on Grafenwerth island. Elegant Art Nouveau houses and parks hark back to the times when kings stayed at this spa. In the picturesque district of Rhöndorf you can visit the house of Konrad Adenauer, where a permanent exhibition presents

the life and times of the first chancellor of the Federal Republic.

Konrad-Adenauer-Strasse 8c
◆ *Tue-Sun 10am-4.30pm (Oct-April), 10am-6pm (May-Sept)*
www.adenauerhaus.de

On the left bank, high on the steep slope of the Rodderberg, the Rolandsbogen (Roland Arch), the only remaining window from Rolandseck Castle points to the next boat pier, at Rolandseck. More than any other monument, the Rolandsbogen symbolises the Romantic era on the Rhine. It was rebuilt following a famous appeal for donations in the *Kölnische Zeitung* newspaper by the young Romantic poet Ferdinand Freiligrath. From Rolandseck you can walk up to the Rolandsbogen and enjoy one of the finest views of the Rhine valley from the terrace of the restaurant. It is also worth visiting the Arp Museum or walking through the wildlife park.

◆ *Wed-Sun 10am-6pm (March-Nov),*
www.wildpark-rolandseck.de

ARP MUSEUM BAHNHOF ROLANDSECK

Especially when seen from the river, the Arp Museum, one of the finest art galleries in the Rhineland, is an impressive sight with its spectacular architecture: a Neoclassical railway station and new building in stylish white by the star architect Richard Meier. Stop off here to enjoy a wonderful view of the "Romantic Rhine" and Siebengebirge, and at the same time to view modern art by Hans Arp and Sophie Taeuber-Arp, one of the most prominent artist couples of the 20th century. Further attractions are exhibitions by international contemporary artists and excellent Old Master paintings from the Rau Collection for UNICEF.

Hans-Arp-Allee 1
◆ *Tue-Sun 11am-6pm*
www.arpmuseum.org

THE BRIDGE AT REMAGEN

Two bridge piers remain today as reminders of the railway bridge that became world-famous through the film of the same name in 1969 about the first crossing of the Rhine by Allied forces. Built in 1918 during the First World War for strategic reasons and named Ludendorff-Brücke, the bridge with a total length of 398 metres was the

place where American forces first crossed the Rhine, on 7 March 1945. Ten days later it collapsed due to the initially unsuccessful German efforts to blow it up and excessive strain. Today the bridge pier on the Remagen side is home to a peace museum, the Friedensmuseum Brücke, while that on the right bank near Erpel is used as a seismographic station.

*Friedensmuseum
Brücke von Remagen*
◆ *10am-6pm (May-Oct),
10am-5pm (Nov-March)
www.bruecke-remagen.de*

The boat passes the little wine town of **Unkel**, where Chancellor Willy Brandt lived, and Schloss Marienfels. On the opposite bank, the pilgrimage church of St Apollinaris, a neo-Gothic building by Zwirner, Cologne Cathedral architect, with frescoes by the Nazarene group of artists heralds the next stop: **Remagen**, worth exploring for its Rhine promenade, Roman remains and the Friedensmuseum.

*Apollinarisberg 4
◆ 9am-6pm (Oct.-Apr.), 9am-
8pm (May-Sep.)
www.apollinariskirche-
remagen.de*

The last stop is Linz, known as the colourful town on the Rhine thanks to its brightly painted half-timbered houses. The attractions here are a visit to Linz Castle with its torture chamber and Roman glass kiln, and a train ride on the Kasbachtal-Bahn to Kalenborn, a steep route past the castle Burg Ockenfels and the Steffens brewery.

◆ *10am-6pm (April-Dec),
Sat-Sun 10am-6pm
(Jan-March)
www.linz-burg.de,
www.zugtouren.de/
Kasbachtalbahn*

Bonn
Beuel
Bundeshaus
Oberkassel
Bad Godesberg · **Königswin**
Rolandseck · **Bad Honnef**
Unkel
Remagen
· **Linz**

Kunst-
museum

City Walk

Born by Night

Government Quarter

Kunstmuseum

3
Days in

Born & Its Surroundings from the River

Strolling and Shopping

BUNDESKUNSTHALLE

Directly opposite the Kunstmuseum, linked to it by Museumsplatz, the Kunst- und Ausstellungshalle (Art and Exhibition Hall) presents highly regarded changing exhibitions about art and culture, technology and science on an area of 5600 square metres. In 1992 the Viennese architect Gustav Peichl designed this square-looking building,

a significant work of architecture and a centre for communication. A conspicuous feature are three pyramids – light wells – on the roof, which is a sculpture garden. 16 steel columns with a dark patina facing Friedrich-Ebert-Allee symbolise the 16 states of the Federal Republic.

Friedrich-Ebert-Allee 4
▲ *Heussallee*
◆ *Tue-Wed 10am-9pm,*
Thu-Sun 10am-7pm
www.bundeskunsthalle.de

RHENISH EXPRESSIONISTS AND GERMAN ART SINCE 1945 – KUNSTMUSEUM BONN

A visit to the Kunstmuseum (Art Museum) shows how light can put life into an art collection, what aims the Rhenish Expressionists pursued, and how German art has developed since 1945.

Before entering, pause for a moment to admire the architecture. The building was designed by Axel Schulte and dates from 1992. Wave and curve shapes, large areas of window glass and irregularly grouped columns characterise the exterior. Inside, the spaces flow into one another, and a theatrical, semi-circular flight of stairs marks

Have a Break

After viewing Expressionist and modern art, try the coffee and cake or other delicacies in the **Café im Kunstmuseum.**
Friedrich-Ebert-Allee 2 ◆ *Tue-Sun 10am-7pm*

the centre. The openness and lighting design make this one of the most significant German museum buildings since the Second World War.

Katharina Grosse's sculpture *In Seven Days Time* stands out next to the entrance. It guides visitors into the museum, where the ground floor is devoted to the art of August Macke. The collection in Bonn, with paintings from all phases of the artist's work, is one of the most comprehensive anywhere, with portraits of his sweetheart Elisabeth, pictures of Bonn and its surroundings, the wild landscape around Lake Thun and the light in Tunis. Works such as *Self-Portrait with a Hat*, *Marienkirche* and *Tightrope Walkers* show how Macke used colour and light as means of composition and expression. He was closely interested in and experimented with the artistic currents of his time, such as Impressionism, Fauvism and Cubism.

On his initiative an exhibition of work by the Rhenish Expressionists was held in 1913. It underlined their aim to be a centre of German art in the west of the country, alongside the groups Die Brücke in Dresden and Berlin, and Blauer Reiter in Munich. From *Märchenwald* by Franz M. Jansen to *Drei Frauen im Grünen* by Hans Thuar, a walk through the collection conveys a good impression of this group of avant-garde artists, who included Heinrich Campendonk, Heinrich Maria Davringhausen, Paul Adolf Seehaus and the young Max Ernst.

3⁞ TIP If the weather is good and the roof garden of the Bundeskunsthalle is open, don't fail to find time to go up there! When the garden is not included in an exhibition, admission is free. Here you can not only see the three roof pyramids, but also visit an airport for birds. This artists' project uses the metaphor of an airport to promote a new attitude to nature. A wildflower meadow, nest boxes, feeders and large structures for taking off and landing encourage birds from all over the world to stop here.

www.bundeskunsthalle.de

MUSEUMSMEILE

If you want to visit the Museum Mile, you have to make choices: natural history in the Museum Alexander König, German history in the Haus der Geschichte, German art in the Kunstmuseum, a major exhibition in the Kunst- und Ausstellungshalle or modern research and technology in the Deutsches Museum: in the space of three kilometres you will find five high-calibre museums here, some of them in impressive new buildings. Each year on the weekend of Corpus Christi, a four-day Museumsmeilenfest presents a programme of art, culture, technology, ecology and open-air attractions.

The second part of the collection, on the upper floor, is dedicated to a completely different theme. Entitled *Wasserstandsmeldung* (literally "Water-Level Report") after an installation by Reinhard Mucha from 1986, this department was rearranged to mark the 20th anniversary of the museum. The rooms are each devoted to one artist in order to illustrate their unmistakable styles, and thus make it possible to trace the varied movements in German art after 1945.

The Graphics Collection is equally fascinating. It includes multiples by Joseph Beuys such as his *Capri Battery*, Max Ernst's artist's books, work on paper by Gerhard Richter and prints by Eduardo Chillida. As these works of art are sensitive to light and can only be displayed for a short time, the collection is presented in constantly changing combinations.

Don't miss the installation entitled *Odeon*, a room-filling, walk-through architectural sculpture by the Munich artist Stefan Eberstadt. There is also a wealth of video art that is probably unequalled in any German museum. Thanks to the collection of the Cologne gallery-owner and patron Ingrid Oppenheim, experimental works by pioneers of video art such as Joan Jonas, Alan Kaprow, Dennis Oppenheim, Peter Campus, Les levine, Klaus vom Bruch, Marcel Odenbach and Ulrike Rosenbach can be seen here.

Friedrich-Ebert-Allee 2
▲ *Heussallee/Museumsmeile*
◆ *Tue, Thu-Sun 11am-6pm, Wed 11am-9pm*
www.kunstmuseum-bonn.de

MUSEUMSMEILE BONN

Accommodation, entertainment, tips and addresses

Hotels

PETERSBERG

... is the name of one of the best-known hills of the Siebengebirge, crowned by a hotel, formerly the guest house of the federal government, where history was made. In 1949 Chancellor Adenauer signed the Petersberg Agreement here. In 1998 the conference of Schengen states was held in the hotel, and in 2001 and 2011 it was the venue for the Afghanistan Conference. Many state guests of the Federal Republic have enjoyed the superb view of the Rhine valley from the 330-metre-high Petersberg and stayed in the elegant rooms of this grand hotel, which is now run by the Steigenberger group. Security could hardly be better, as only one access road winds up the hill in hairpin bends.

www.steigenberger.com/ Koenigswinter_Bonn

LOW BUDGET

● **MAX HOSTEL**
Maxstrasse 7 (Old Town)
Tel. 0228/82345780
▲ Stadthaus
www.max-hostel.de

Low-cost accommodation in a quiet location in the heart of the Old Town.

● **IBIS BONN****
Vorgebirgsstrasse 33 (City Centre)
Tel. 0228/72660
▲ Frankenbad/Kunstverein
www.ibishotel.com

Reasonably priced hotel near the shopping zone with free WiFi in the lobby.

SUPERIOR

● **AMERON HOTEL KÖNIGSHOF****
Adenauerallee 9 (City Centre)
Tel. 0228/26010
▲ Universität/Markt
www.hotel-koenigshof-bonn.de

Elegant 4-star superior right on the Rhine conveniently situated for shopping and the business district.

● **BEST WESTERN HOTEL DOMICIL****
Thomas-Mann-Strasse 24-26
Tel. 0228/729090
▲ Poppelsdorfer Allee
www.bestwestern.de

Business hotel in Art Deco style near the main railway station.

● **DERAG LIVINGHOTEL KANZLER****
Adenauerallee 148 (Südstadt)
Tel. 0228/68440
▲ Museum Koenig
www.deraghotels.de

Here on the Museum Mile you can choose between a hotel room, an apartment and a suite.

● **DORINT HOTEL VENUSBERG BONN****
An der Casselsruhe 1 (Venusberg)
Tel. 0228/2880
▲ Casselruhe
hotel-bonn.dorint.com

Stylish address in the middle of a nature park, but only a few minutes away from the centre of Bonn.

Kameha Grand Bonn

● **INSEL HOTEL***+**
Theaterplatz 5-7
(Bad Godesberg)
Tel. 0228-35000
▲ Bad Godesberg Bahnhof
www.inselhotel.com

Modern hotel in the centre of Bad Godesberg near the spa park.

● **MARITIM HOTEL BONN****
Godesberger Allee
(Bad Godesberg)
Tel. 0228/81080
▲ Olof-Palme-Allee/ Deutsche Telekom, Robert-Schuman-Platz
www.maritim.de

Near the park on the Rhine and the Museum Mile between Bonn and Bad Godesberg, this exclusive hotel is suitable for business people and weekenders.

● **MY POPPELSDORF*****
Wallfahrtsweg 4
(Poppelsdorf)
Tel. 0228/26910
▲ Poppelsdorfer Platz
www.mypoppelsdorf.com

Small modern hotel without a restaurant in Poppelsdorf.

● **STERNHOTEL*****
Markt 8 (City Centre)
Tel. 0228/72670
▲ Uni/Markt
www.sternhotel-bonn.de

Old-established, architecturally attractive hotel right on the marketplace and close to the historic town hall.

DELUXE

● **KAMEHA GRAND BONN******
Am Bonner Bogen 1
(Ramersdorf)
Tel. 0228/43345000
▲ Konrad-Zuse-Platz, Bahnhof Oberkassel
www.kamehagrand.com

Luxury hotel with stand-out architecture and interior design on the right bank of the river Rhine, a member of the Leading Hotels of the World group.

● **STEIGENBERGER GRANDHOTEL PETERSBERG******
Petersberg (Königswinter)
Tel. 02223/740
▲ Bahnhof Königswinter
www.steigenberger.com/ Koenigswinter_Bonn

Grand hotel with an extremely high level of comfort, and an aura of history about it.

WORLD CONFERENCE CENTER

The former plenary assembly chamber of the Deutscher Bundestag and the Wasserwerk have been used as a congress centre since parliament moved to Berlin. In close proximity to the United

Nations Campus, Deutsche Welle, the headquarters of Deutsche Post DHL, ministries and international organisations, the World Conference Center Bonn has facilities for all kinds of events for up to 1270 persons. Since the completion of an extension and the attached hotel, up to 7000 persons can be accommodated.

www.worldccbonn.com

SERVICE

Restaurants

BÖNNSCHE SPEZIALITÄTEN

Äppelschloot
Potato salad

Brootwoosch
Fried or grilled sausage

Hämmche met Stampes un suurem Kappes
Pork knuckle with mashed potatoes and sauerkraut

Halve Hahn
"Half a chicken" – actually a rye-bread roll with medium-mature Gouda cheese, butter and mustard

Himmel un Äd
Fried blood sausage with mashed potato and apple sauce

● **COSI**
Prinz-Albert-Strasse 42
(Südstadt)
Tel. 0228/3362536
▲ Königstrasse
◆ Mon-Sat noon-2.30pm,
6-10.30pm

Bonners love this nice little Italian restaurant for its plain, down-to-earth cooking and reasonable prices.

● **HALBEDEL**
Rheinallee 47
(Bad Godesberg)
Tel. 0228/354253
▲ Otto-Kühne-Schule
◆ Tue-Sun 6pm-midnight
www.halbedel.de

Michelin-starred gourmet restaurant in wonderful Art Nouveau surroundings.

● **PASTIS**
Rheingasse 5
(City Centre)
Tel. 0228/9694270
▲ Universität/Markt
◆ Tue-Sun noon-8pm
www.hotel-pastis.de

Those who love French cuisine can enjoy it in a casual atmosphere in this bistro near the opera.

● **LA CIGALE**
Friedrichstrasse 18
(City Centre)
▲ Beethovenhaus
◆ Mon-Thu noon-3pm,
6-10pm,
Fri-Sat noon-11pm
lacigale.de

With oysters and bouillabaisse you can enjoy a touch of French savoir-vivre and Parisian style at the heart of Bonn.

● **MATTHIEU'S**
Argelanderstrasse 103
(Poppelsdorf)
Tel. 0228/2891229
▲ Wilhelm-Levison-Strasse
◆ Mon, Wed-Fri noon-3pm,
6-10pm, Sat-Sun 5pm-1am
www.matthieus.de

Modern German cooking with Mediterranean influence is on the menu here, produced according to the motto "cooking is an art form, and by no means the least important".

NEES
Meckenheimer Allee 169
(in Botanical Garden)
▲ Am Botanischen Garten
◆ Tue-Sat noon-midnight
www.nees-bonn.de

Fine Dining in the Botanical Garden!

● **OLIVETO**
Adenauerallee 9 (City Centre)
Tel. 0228/311296
▲ Universität/Markt
◆ 6.30-10.30am, noon-2.30pm, 6-10pm
www.hotel-koenigshof-bonn.de

Regarded as the best Italian in Bonn, popular for its wonderful terrace with a view of the Rhine.

● **IL PUNTO**
Lennèstrasse 6
(City Centre)
▲ Universität/Markt
◆ Fri-Wed noon-2.30pm, 6-10.30pm
www.ilpunto.de

For some 30 years the proprietor, Ettore, has been providing high-class Italian cuisine.

● **RINCON DE ESPAÑA**
Karthäuserplatz 21
(Kessenich)
Tel. 0228/239609
▲ Pützstrasse
◆ Tue-Thu 5pm-midnight, Fr 5pm-1am, Sat noon-1am, Sun noon-midnight
www.ristorante-sassella.de

Old-established Spanish restaurant, a Bonn institution, known for more than its tapas. In summer guests dine outdoors beneath old chestnut trees.

● **ROSES**
Martinsplatz 2a
Tel. 0228/4330653
▲ Hauptbahnhof
◆ from 9am
www.roses-bonn.de

With a view of the minster – in summer on the terrace – you can sample Mediterranean food, or round off the evening at the bar by the fireplace.

● **STRANDHAUS**
Georgstrasse 28
(Old Town)
Tel. 0228/3694949
▲ Kölnstrasse
◆ Tue-Sat 6-1am
www.strandhaus-bonn.de

Good-quality, varied seasonal food is served in this restaurant in the Old Town.

● **TERRA VINO**
Hubertinumshof 11
(Bad Godesberg)
Tel. 0228/3297858
▲ Bad Godesberg Bf./Rheinallee
◆ Mon-Sat 11.30am-3pm, 6pm-midnight
www.terra-vino.de

In this Italian wine shop and delicatessen you can also dine on wonderful Sicilian food.

BÖNNSCHE SPEZIALITÄTEN

Kölsche Kaviar
A slice of blood sausage with onion rings

Öllichzupp
Onion soup

Prummetaart
Plum cake

Quallmänner
Potatoes boiled in their skin

Rievkoche
Rösti potatoes/potato fritters

Soorbrode
Sour-marinated beef or horsemeat

Cafés, Pubs & Beer Gardens

BONN CALENDAR

FEBRUARY:
Weiberfastnacht in Beuel, parade on Carnival Monday
www.kamelle.de

APRIL:
Easter fair on the Rhine bank in Beuel
www.bonnarge.de

Rheinaue flea market
www.flohmarkt-rheinaue.de

Deutsche Post Marathon Bonn
www.deutschepost-marathonbonn.de

MAY:
The Rhine in Flames
www.rhein-in-flammen.com

EUREGA
www.eurega.org

Bonsai exhibition in the Rheinaue

Macke-Viertel-Fest

Night of the Churches
www.bonnerkirchennacht.de

Theatre Night
www.bonnertheatemacht.de

JUNE:
Balloon Festival
www.ballonfestival-bonn.de

Museum Mile Festival

Prix Pantheon
www.pantheon.de

Science Night
www.bonner-wissenschaftsnacht.de

● ALTER ZOLL
Am Brassertufer
▲ Universität/Markt
◆ 11am-midnight (summer)

Beautiful beer garden right by the Rhine next to the university.

● BRAUHAUS BÖNNSCH
Sterntorbrücke 4 (City Centre)
▲ Friedensplatz
◆ Mon-Thu 11am-1am, Fri-Sat 11am-3am, Sun 12 noon-1am
www.boennsch.de

Come here for beer brewed on site and Rhineland food.

● BON(N) GOUT
Remigiusplatz 2-4
▲ Thomas-Mann-Strasse, Stadthaus
◆ Mon-Thu 9am-11pm, Fri-Sat 9am-midnight, Sun 10am-9pm
www.bonngout.com

In this attractive café by the flower market, a place for people-watching, you can try home-made cakes or Mediterranean cooking.

● CAFÉ GIACOMO
Bottlerplatz 10 (City Centre)
▲ Stadthaus
◆ Sun-Thu 9am-1am, Fri-Sat 9am-2am
www.cafe-giaccomo.de

Whether you come for a stylish French breakfast or to while away the evening with champagne or delicious cocktails, Café Giacomo is a fine place at any time of day.

● MEYER'S
Clemens-August-Strasse 51 (Poppelsdorf)
▲ Poppelsdorfer Platz
◆ Mon-Sat from 5.30pm, Sun from 10am, Brunch 10am-2.30pm (winter)
www.meyers-bonn.de

An attractive mix of pub and restaurant in Poppelsdorf for everyone who enjoys cosy surroundings and creative cuisine.

● MIDI
Münsterplatz 11
▲ Thomas-Mann-Strasse, Stadthaus
◆ 9am–midnight
www.midi-bonn.de

A great place to drink latte macchiato on Münsterplatz, outdoors if the sun shines or indoors in the converted dairy.

● **PAWLOW**
Heerstrasse 64 (Nordstadt)
▲ Stadthaus
◆ Sun-Thu 10-2am, Fri-Sat
10-5am

Trendy pub with sunny out-door seating in the Old Town. Known for its café au lait in the morning and music in the evenings.

● **PATHOS**
Weberstrasse 43 (Südstadt)
▲ Weberstrasse
◆ 10am-1am
www.cafe-pathos.com

A wonderful corner pub with a beer garden, where you can eat a snack with your beer.

● **RHEINLUST**
Rheinaustrasse 134
(Beuel)
◆ Mon-Thu 10-1am,
Fri-Sat 10-3am,
Sun 9-1am

A beer garden right opposite the opera house where guests, who are not only students, have a wonderful view of the sunset.

● **ROHMÜHLE**
Rheinwerkallee 3
(Ramersdorf)
▲ Ramersdorf
◆ Mon-Sat 10am-11pm
Sun from 9.30am
www.rohmuehle.net

A trip out to this beautiful terrace on the banks of the Rhine in Oberkassel next to the Kameha Grand is well worthwhile, not only for the view of Bonn and the Siebengebirge.

● **SCHAUMBURGER HOF**
Am Schaumburger Hof 10
(Plittersdorf)
▲ Steinhaus
◆ Tue-Sun noon-10pm

A lovely beer garden where you can sit beneath lime trees by the historic inn to enjoy a cooling drink and delicious food, with a view of the Rhine and Sieben-gebirge including the Drachenfels and Petersberg.

● **SCHLOSS-CAFÉ**
Clemens-August-Strasse 21
(Poppelsdorf)
▲ Poppelsdorfer Platz
◆ 7.30am-5pm
schloss-cafe-poppelsdorf.de

The best cakes in Bonn are here!

● **STRANDBAR
AM RHEINPAVILLON**
Rathenauufer 1 (City Centre)
▲ Juridicum
◆ 10am-9pm (depending on the weather and level of the river)
www.strandbar-bonn.de

This beach bar on the banks of the Rhine gives you the holiday feeling. If the weather is not fine, the restaurant and terrace of the Rheinpavillon are a good alternative.

BONN CALENDAR

JULY:
Beer Festival
www.bierboerse.com

AUGUST:
International Silent Film Festival
www.internationale-stummfilmtage.de

SEPTEMBER:
Beethovenfest
www.beethovenfest.de

Company run
www.firmenlauf-bonn.de

Pützchens Markt
www.puetzchens-markt.de

Bonn-Fest

OCTOBER:
Klangwelle music festival
www.klangwelle-bonn.de

Pantheon A Cappella-Festival
www.pantheon.de

NOVEMBER:
Start of Carnival season
www.kamelle.de

DECEMBER:

Christmas market on Münsterplatz
www.bonnerweihnachts-markt.de

Bars & Nightlife

BONN'S VITAL STATISTICS

Home to almost 325,000 inhabitants, the Federal City of Bonn is one of the ten largest cities in North-Rhine Westphalia, and one of the oldest in Germany with a history going back 2000 years. Some 25 per cent of the population of Bonn are immigrants or from immigrant families. About 42 per cent are Roman Catholic, 23.5 are Protestant and 9.1 per cent Muslim.

The city boundary has a length of 61 kilometres. The area of Bonn is maximum 12.5 kilometres from west to east and 15 kilometres from north to south. It measures over 141 square kilometres, of which almost 45 per cent is built-up or used for traffic, 17 per cent is used for agriculture, and 28 per cent is woodland.

Bonn lies at the transition from the slate hills of the mid-Rhine to the plain of the lower Rhine.

● BELLINI
Rathausgasse 38
(City Centre)
▲ Universität/Markt
◆ Sun-Thu 6pm-3am,
Fri-Sat 6pm-5am
www.bar-bellini.com

A place for cool people, where politicians and journalists used to meet when Bonn was capital city.

● BLOW UP
Rathausgasse 10
(City Centre)
▲ Universität/Markt
◆ 22-5am
www.blow-up-bonn.de

This former strip club is now a trendy pub with a couch and dance floor. DJs make music each evening, in different styles.

● CARPE NOCTEM
Wesselstrasse 5
(City Centre)
▲ Hauptbahnhof or Universität/Markt
See www.carpe-noctem-bonn.de for the programme

A student club and local institution. Both the music and the clientele are diverse.

● CHE GUEVARA
Münsterstrasse 9
(City Centre)
▲ Hauptbahnhof
◆ Mon-Thu 5pm-1am,
Fri-Sat 5pm-3am
www.cheguevara-bonn.de

Lots of delicious cocktails are shaken in this little bar, not least mojito and daiquiri.

● CLUB N8SCHICHT
Bornheimer Strasse 20-22
(Nordstadt)
▲ Stadthaus
◆ Wed-Sat 10pm-5am
www.n8schicht.de

A party location with something to suit every taste.

● DAS SOFA
Maximilianstrasse 8
(City Centre)
▲ Hauptbahnhof
See www.sofa-bonn.de for the programme

This night club puts on karaoke, readings by authors, comedy and themed parties.

● JAZZ GALERIE BONN
Oxfordstrasse 24
(City Centre)
▲ Bertha-von-Suttner-Platz/ Beethovenhaus
See www.jazzgalerie-bonn.de for the programme

A veteran of Bonn's nightlife – not only for jazz, but also for various party events.

● **MOJITO**
Königstrasse 9 (Südstadt)
▲ Königstrasse
◆ from 6pm
www.mojito-bonn.de

Cosy little cocktail bar serving Spanish tapas as well as its speciality, mojito.

● **OXFORD BAR**
Oxfordstrasse 19D
▲ Stadthaus
◆ Fri-Sat 8pm-3am, Sun 10.30pm-5am
www.oxfordbar.com

A stylish bar with high-class drinks!

● **PIANOBAR**
(in the Maritim Hotel Bonn)
Godesberger Allee
(Bad Godesberg)

▲ Olof-Palme-Allee/
Deutsche Telekom,
Robert-Schuman-Platz
◆ Mon-Sat from 6pm

Classic hotel bar with live music.

● **SHAKER'S**
Bornheimer Strasse 26
(City Centre)
▲ Stadthaus
◆ Mon-Tue 5pm-midnight,
Wed-Thu, 5pm-1am,
Fri-Sat 3pm-3am,
Sun 4pm-midnight
www.shakers-bonn.de

Has a long-standing reputation as Bonn's best bar. The barkeepers put on an impressive show of shaking cocktails, and DJs lay on the music on warm summer nights.

Its highest point is the Paffelsberg in Ennert at 194.8 metres, its lowest the point the mouth of the river Sieg at 45.6 metres above sea level. Its tallest structure is the Venusberg TV antenna at 180 metres, followed by the 163-metre Post-Tower. Following the departure of the German parliament and part

of the government, Bonn has successfully adapted and is an attractive location for employers thanks to the close links between business and science. In addition to two Dax-listed corporations, Deutsche Post DHL and Deutsche Telekom, almost 16,000 small and medium-sized companies are based in Bonn. 18 branches of the United Nations make it an important base for international organisations, and the unique combination of scientific institutions makes it a significant centre for research. The completion of the World Conference Center will consolidate Bonn's reputation as a venue for conferences.

Spas and Fitness

ARBORETUM HÄRLE

When Franz Carl Rennen, the director of a railway company, planted Atlas cedars, a gingko and a redwood at his summer residence in 1870, he could not have known that this was the beginning a beautiful landscaped park. Thanks to its favourable climate on a slope of the Rhine valley, the arboretum is now a park with extensive plant collections, many kinds of roses, valuable individual plants and extremely rare trees. It is managed by a charitable foundation that was established by the daughters of the later owner, Carl Härle. Guided tours take visitors to the Alter Park (old park) with its Bauhaus-style residences, the Neuer Park (new park) on the site of the former nursery, and the Waldpark (wooded park) with a lake and orchard.

Büchelstrasse 40 (Oberkassel)
Visits only as part of a guided tour:
www.arboretum-haerle.de

● **FLOATING CENTER BONN**
in Massagepraxis
Karin Becker
Estermannstrasse 91
(Graurheindorf)
Tel. 0228/24267403
▲ Werftstrasse
◆ 1-9pm
www.floating-in-bonn.de

Give body and soul some time out and relax by drifting in the salt water of the floating tank.

● **MONTE MARE**
Münstereifeler Strasse 6
53359 Rheinbach
Tel. 02226/90300
▲ Bahnhof Rheinbach
(regional train to Münstereifel)
◆ Mon-Thu 9am-11pm,
Fri-Sat 9am-midnight,
Sun 9am-9pm
www.monte-mare.de

Take a day's holiday near Bonn to get back your strength in the sauna or through spa treatments.

Juba Wellness Tempel

● **JUBA WELLNESS TEMPEL**
in the Derag Livinghotel Kanzler
Adenauerallee 148
Tel. 0228/3692442 und 3692422
▲ Museum Koenig,
Bundeskanzlerplatz
◆ Mon, Wed-Thu 12 noon-10pm, Fri-Sun 10am-9pm
www.jubawellnesstempel.de

For a massage or hammam, a steam bath or a sauna, here you can enjoy a relaxing break.

● **SALZGROTTE VITAL**
Siegburger Strasse 54
(Beuel)
Tel. 0228/96397429
▲ Schauspielhalle
◆ Mon-Sat 10am-8pm,
Sun noon-8pm
www.beuel-vital.de

Spoil yourself for a day with Thai massage and cosmetic treatments, and perhaps a spell in the healthy salt grotto.

● **SAUNAPARK SIEBENGEBIRGE**
Dollendorfer Strasse 106-110
(Königswinter-Oberpleis)
Tel. 02244/921714
▲ Am Auel/Freizeit-Zentrum (bus 537 from Bonn)
◆ Mon-Thu 11am-11pm, Fri 11am-midnight, Sat 10pm-midnight, Sun 10am-10pm
www.saunapark-siebengebirge.de

In the Saunapark you can take a break from the everyday routine, with a choice between the swimming pool, sauna, spa and massage treatments.

● **SPORTFABRIK**
Auguststrasse 32 (Beuel)
Tel. 0228/403690
◆ Mon-Fri 7-11pm, Sat-Sun 9am-10pm
www.sportfabrik.de

Spend some time in the Roman sauna village, and then chill out on the beach terrace with a wonderful view of Bonn.

● **WELLFITPARK**
Mallwitzstrasse 24
(Bad Godesberg)
Tel. 0228/333000
◆ Mon, Wed, Fri 8am-11pm, Tue, Thu 7am-11pm, Sat-Sun 9am-8pm
www.wellfitpark.com

Here you can do good for your body and soul: there are a sauna, pool, tennis courts and massage treatment rooms all under one roof.

● **KAMEHA SPA POWER HOUSE**
(at Kameha Grand Bonn)
Am Bonner Bogen 1
(Ramersdorf)
Tel. 0228/43345400
▲ Konrad-Zuse-Platz
◆ Mon-Thu 7am-midnight, Fri-Sun 7am-10pm
www.kamehagrand.com/de/spa-powerhouse

In the rooftop pool enjoy a unique view of the Rhine and Bonn while taking high-quality treatments.

RHEINAUE

If you are looking for an oasis of greenery, after visiting the government quarter take a walk through a park that is almost as big as the centre of Bonn. On both sides of the Rhine lies a recreational area of 160 hectares that was once used for the federal garden show. 45 kilometres of paths for walking and

cycling criss-cross a terrain with riverside woodland, meadows and much more. Popular places here are the Auensee lake, where you can hire a boat, and the Japanese Garden, where a 13-storey pagoda stands.

Ludwig-Erhardt-Allee (Gronau),
▲ *Heussallee*

Derag Livinghotel Kanzler

Culture

BEETHOVEN ORCHESTRA

For over 100 years the Beethoven-Orchester has been Bonn's cultural ambassador, giving concerts on tour in Germany and abroad. Today it is one of the leading German orchestras. When it was founded in 1907, the city gained a professional orchestra for the first time since the disbandment of the prince elector's court orchestra in 1794. It has performed under such famous composers and conductors as Richard Strauss, Paul Hindemith and Kurt Masur.

The ensemble has borne the name of the city's most famous son only since 2003. Today, led by Dirk Kaftan, its general director of music, the orchestra has a major role in the cultural life of Bonn by playing at the Beethoven Festival, in the Beethovenhalle and at the opera house.

www.beethoven-orchester.de

MUSIC

● **BEETHOVENHALLE**
Wachsbleiche 16
Tel. 0228/72220
▲ Beethovenhalle
www.beethovenhalle.de

The municipal concert hall hosts performances by the Beethoven Orchestra and world-famous international ensembles and soloists.

● **HARMONIE**
Frongasse 28-30 (Endenich)
Tel. 0228/614042
▲ Auf dem Hügel
www.harmonie-bonn.de

Music club with a pub and beer garden attached, putting on a wide range of jazz, blues and rock concerts.

● **KLASSISCHE PHILHARMONIE BONN**
Belderberg 24
Tel. 0228/654965
www.klassische-philharmonie-bonn.de

A touring concert orchestra with an international reputation for its Vienna Classics subscription series.

● **OPERNHAUS/WERKSTATT**
Am Boeselagerhof 1
Tel. 0228/778000
▲ Bertha-von-Suttner-Platz
www.theater-bonn.de

The programme of the opera house next to the Kennedybrücke ranges from the classic opera repertoire and dance to contemporary works.

3 TIP Take a look at the programme of KUNST!RASEN! In summer fantastic concerts are held in the open air between the former Deutscher Bundestag and the DHL/Post-Tower, right by the Rhine.
www.kunstrasen-bonn.de

THEATER & KABARETT

● **BROTFABRIK THEATER gGMBH**
Kreuzstrasse 16
Tel. 0228/43368070
▲ Obere Wilhelmstrasse, Konrad Adenauer-Platz
www.theater.brotfabrik-bonn.de

Arts centre for performances of world music, drama and dance.

● **CONTRA-KREIS-THEATER**
Am Hof 3-5 (City Centre)
Tel. 0228/632307
▲ Universität/Markt
www.contra-kreis-theater.de

Bonn's oldest private theatre for comedy and farce, next to the university, is known beyond the Bonn region for its premieres.

● **EURO THEATER CENTRAL BONN**
Münsterplatz-Dreieck
Entrance on Mauspfad
Tel. 0228/652951
▲ Hauptbahnhof
www.eurotheater.de

An intimate studio theatre, with a stage measuring only 38 square metres and seats for 50 spectators at most, which has put on legendary performances of Patrick Süskind's *The Double Bass* and Sartre's *No Exit (Huits Clos)*.

● **HALLE BEUEL/ALTER MALERSAAL/LAMPENLAGER**
Siegburger Strasse 42 (Beuel)
Tel. 0228/778407
▲ Schauspielhalle Beuel
www.theater-bonn.de

The studio theatre of the municipal ensemble in what used to be a jute-spinning factory.

● **JUNGES THEATER BONN**
Hermannstr. 50 (City Centre)
Tel. 0228/463672
▲ Beuel Krankenhaus
www.jt-bonn.de

A children's theatre with an excellent reputation and more than 40 years' experience.

● **KAMMERSPIELE**
Am Michaelshof 9 (Bad Godesberg)
Tel. 0228/7780022
▲ Bad Godesberg Bahnhof/Rheinallee
www.theater-bonn.de

The main venue of the city theatre ensemble with a repertoire of classics and contemporary works.

PRIX PANTHEON

This is a major event on the German cabaret scene, whether you experience it live in Bonn's Pantheon theatre or on television. The Prix

Pantheon is one of the leading awards for satirical cabaret, nicely subtitled the "German Fun and Satire Open". Twelve artists or groups from the categories cabaret, comedy, a capella and chansons are invited to present their talents to the audience live on three evenings, competing for a jury award (named "precocious but gone off") and an audience award ("applauded and booed"). The winners of the special awards "mature and mad" and "giving and taking" are known in advance. The cabaret artist Rainer Pause, founder of the Pantheon, presents the awards, which he established in 1995.

www.pantheon.de

Culture

SPRINGMAUS

A word, a theme or a song – called out by a member of the audience – is all that is needed for the artists at Springmaus ("jumping mouse") to act out a scene. This is improvised theatre in its purest form, and has made this ensemble in Bonn famous all over Germany. Founded in 1983 by the Canadian actor Bill Mockridge, the ensemble started out playing in the table-tennis cellar of a Catholic youth club. Soon big names in satire and cabaret were appearing

Haus der SPRINGMAUS

here, and some well-known names started their careers on the Springmaus stage. Since 1993 the jumping mice have had their own house, a dance hall from the early 20th century on the Kulturmeile in Endenich. Their own productions and performances by guest artists are staged there.

Tickets 0228/798081
www.springmaus-theater.de

● **KLEINES THEATER BAD GODESBERG**
Koblenzer Strasse 78
(Bad Godesberg)
0228/362839
▲ Stadthalle
www.kleinestheater-badgodesberg.de

All kinds of offerings are staged here in the old mayor's house by the spa park – from classical drama, established modern plays, tragedies and popular comedies to opera and musicals.

● **PANTHEON THEATER**
Bundeskanzlerplatz 2-10
Tel. 0228/212521
▲ Bundeskanzlerplatz, Museum König, Heussallee
www.pantheon.de

One of Germany's leading cabaret theatres. Up-and-coming artists and established stars present political satire and more. The Pantheon Casino in the Bonn-Center is a new second venue!

● **THEATER DIE PATHOLOGIE**
Weberstrasse 43 (Südstadt)
Tel. 0228/222358
▲ Weberstrasse
www.theaterdiepathologie.de

Bonn's smallest and cosiest theatre, with just 25 seats in the "catacombs" of Café Pathos, puts on contemporary and experimental theatre, as well as dramatisations of themes from world literature.

● **theaterimballsaal**
Frongasse 9 (Endenich)
Tel. 0228/797901
▲ Brahmsstrasse
www.theater-im-ballsaal.de

An independent theatre that is run by two groups: fringe ensemble (theatre) and CocoonDance (dance).

KINOS

● **CINESTAR BONN STERNLICHTSPIELE**
Markt 8-10, Bonn
Tel. 01805/118811
▲ Rathaus, Bertha-von-Suttner-Platz
www.cinestar.de

All the latest films are screened here.

● **BONNER KINEMATHEK**
Kreuzstrasse 16
(by the Brotfabrik/Beuel)
Tel. 0228/478489

▲ Konrad-Adenauer-Platz
www.bonnerkinemathek.de

Ambitious programme of art-house films, usually shown in the original language.

● **KINOPOLIS**
Moltkestrasse 7-9
(Bad Godesberg)
Tel. 0228/830083
▲ Moltkestrasse, Plittersdorfer Strasse
www.kinopolis.de

A multiplex cinema with the latest Hollywood movies.

● **NEUE FILMBÜHNE**
Friedrich-Breuer-Strasse 68-70 (Beuel)
Tel. 0228/469790
▲ Beuel Rathaus, Konrad Adenauer Platz
www.rex-filmbuehne.de

A venue for art-house movies, premieres and repertoire cinema with 1930s architecture.

● **REX LICHTSPIELTHEATER**
Frongasse 9 (Endenich)
Tel. 0228/622330
▲ Frongasse
www.rex-filmbuehne.de

Old-established cinema in the Endenich cultural quarter, which often shows premieres of German and European films.

● **WOKI-FILMPALAST AND ATELIER**
Bertha-von-Suttner-Platz 1-7
Tel. 0228/9768200
▲ Bertha-von-Suttner-Platz
www.woki.de

Here the German premieres of blockbusters are screened at moderate prices, older films at very low prices.

ERNST ROBERT CURTIUS PRIZE

In honour of the scholar Ernst Robert Curtius (1886–1956), who taught at Bonn University from 1913 to 1920 and was one of the most important German experts on Romance languages and literature, in 1984 Thomas Grundmann, a bookseller and publisher from Bonn, sponsored an award for essays. This literary prize is presented every two years by the Universitätsgesellschaft Bonn for an essayist's life's work or for an outstanding individual work, with the intention of promoting German-language essays as an independent literary genre and, in memory of Curtius, strengthening the common European spirit. Since 1986 a second Ernst Robert Curtius Prize has been awarded to writers below the age of 40.

SERVICE

Museums

LANDESMUSEUM

Whether you come to see the 42,000-year-old skeleton of a Neanderthal, the Celtic bronze helmet from Flüren, the gravestone of Marcus Caelius, the choir screens from Gustorf or J.M.W. Turner's *Cross and Godesburg*, in this museum you can immerse yourself in the artistic and cultural history of the Rhineland. Artistic masterpieces and everyday items, religious works and simple tools illustrate the life of people in the Rhineland from the Stone Age to the present day, presenting them according to themes such as religion, environment, technology and luxury.

Colmantstrasse 14-16 (City Centre)
▲ *Hauptbahnhof*
◆ *Tue-Fri, Sun 11am-6pm, Sat 1-6pm*
www.rlmb.lvr.de/museum

● **ÄGYPTISCHES MUSEUM DER UNIVERSITÄT BONN**
Regina-Pacis-Weg 7 (City Centre)
▲ Universität/Markt
◆ Tue-Fri 1-5pm, Sat-Sun 1-6pm
www.aegyptisches-museum.uni-bonn.de

Some 700 exhibits in the collection of the Egyptian Museum present an interesting picture of the civilisation of ancient Egypt.

● **AKADEMISCHES KUNSTMUSEUM**
➤ p. 19

● **ARITHMEUM**
Lennéstrasse 2
▲ Universität/Markt
◆ Tue-Sun 11am-6pm
www.arithmeum.uni-bonn.de

With its motto "calculating in the past and present", the museum initiates a dialogue between science and art.

● **BEETHOVEN-HAUS**
➤ p. 64

● **BONNER KUNSTVEREIN**
Hochstadenring 22-24 (Nordstadt)

▲ Bonn West
◆ Tue-Wed, Fri-Sun 11am-5pm, Thu 11am-7pm
www.bonner-kunstverein.de

The Bonn Art Society presents themed exhibitions on major trends in contemporary art and individual shows of the work of outstanding international artists.

● **DEUTSCHES MUSEUM BONN**
Ahrstrasse 45 (in the Wissenschaftszentrum/Plittersdorf)
▲ Hochkreuz/Deutsches Museum Bonn
◆ Tue-Sun 10am-6pm
www.deutsches-museum.de/bonn

100 exhibits exemplify the subject "research and technology in Germany since 1945".

● **FRAUENMUSEUM**
Im Krausfeld 10 (City Centre)
▲ Rosental
◆ Tue-Sat 2-6pm,
Sun 11am-6pm
www.frauenmuseum.de

Since 1981 the world's
first museum of this
kind has been showing
the variety of female
creativity.

● **HAUS DER GESCHICHTE**
➤ p. 33

● **HORST-STOECKEL-MUSEUM**
Sigmund-Freud-Strasse 25
▲ Kliniken Nord
◆ Mon-Fri 9am-1.30pm
www.anaesthesie-museum.uni-bonn.de

One of four internationally
significant museums pre-
sents the history of anaes-
thesiology.

● **KUNST- UND AUSSTELLUNGSHALLE DER BUNDESREPUBLIK DEUTSCHLAND**
➤ p. 46

● **KUNSTMUSEUM BONN**
➤ p. 45

● **MINERALOGISCHES MUSEUM AM STEINMANN-INSTITUT DER UNIVERSITÄT BONN**
Poppelsdorfer Schloss,
Meckenheimer Allee 169
(Südstadt)
◆ Wed+Fri 3-6pm,
Sun 10am-5pm
www.steinmann.uni-bonn.de/museen/mineralogisches-museum

One of Germany's leading
mineralogical collections.

● **MUSEUM ALEXANDER KOENIG**
➤ p. 26

● **STADTMUSEUM BONN**
Franziskanerstrasse 9
(City Centre)
▲ Universität/Markt
◆ Wed 9.30am-2pm,
Thu-Sat 1-6pm,
Sun 11.30am-5pm
www2.bonn.de/stadtmuseum

Every aspect of the history
of Bonn.

AUGUST-MACKE-HAUS

The house in which the
painter August Macke
lived with his family
from 1910 until his early
death in 1914, a rendez-
vous for the Rhineland
art scene where artists
such as Robert Delaunay
and Guillaume Apol-
linaire, Franz Marc and
Gabriele Münter came
and went, is today a
centre for Rhenish

Expressionism. It is
also a museum, where
Macke's studio can
be visited. The view
through the window
here provided him with
many of his motifs, such
as the Marienkirche and
Kreuzbergkirche church-
es, and flower gardens.
Changing exhibitions
also cast light on the
life and work of the art-
ist and his circle.

*Bornheimer Strasse 96
(Nordstadt)*
▲ *Heerstrasse,
Eifelstrasse*
◆ *Reopening in autumn
2017*
www.august-macke-haus.de

Shopping

PÜTZCHENS MARKT

On the second weekend in September each year, the historic centre and meadows of Pützchen in the district of Beuel are transformed for six days into a gigantic fair, with rides, snack bars, beer stalls and much more. The traditional opening of Pützchens Markt is a service in the church of St Adelheid, as the fair owes its existence to this saint. According to a legend, she discovered a spring (in the Rhineland

dialect Pütz, or Pützchen) during a drought in about the year 1000. This spring soon became a place of pilgrimage, and in the 14th century a market with clothing, inn-keepers, and jugglers and other performers arose for the benefit of pilgrims. Over the centuries it developed into a big fair.

www.puetzchens-markt.de

● ART DECO
Martinsplatz 2a/Kaiser-passage (City Centre)
▲ Universität/Markt
◆ Mon–Fri 11am–6.30pm, Sat 10am–4pm
www.art-deco-schaefer.de

Attractive for purchasers and window-shoppers: here you find art and costume jewellery from the 1920s to the 1950s.

● BUCHCAFÉ ANTIQUARIUS
Bonner Talweg 14 (Südstadt)
▲ Weberstrasse
◆ Tue-Sat 10am-8pm
www.buch-antiquarius.de

Drink wine or coffee while browsing in a second-hand bookshop.

● COPPENEUR-CHOCOLATIER
Friedrichstrasse 56 (City Centre)
▲ Bertha-von-Suttner-Platz/Beethoven-Haus
◆ Mon-Fri 10am-7pm, Sat 10am-6pm
www.coppeneur.de

Heaven for chocoholics, with a big selection of pralines, truffles and chocolate.

● DER KLEINE LADEN
Friedrich-Breuer-Strasse 52 (Beuel)
▲ Konrad-Adenauer-Platz
◆ Mon-Fri 10am-6.30pm, Sat 10am-2pm
www.derkleineladen-bonn.de

Lots of presents for old and young.

● GLOBETROTTER OUTLET
Vorgebirgsstrasse 86 (Nordstadt)
▲ Bonn West
◆ Mon-Sat 10am-8pm
www.globetrotter.de

Fans of outdoor activities come here in search of bargains.

● HAUS DER MUSIK
Wenzelgasse 13 (City Centre)
▲ Bertha-von-Suttner-Platz/Beethoven-Haus
◆ Mon-Fri 10am-6.30pm, Sat 10am-4pm
www.haus-der-musik.net

Family-run for four generations, this store sells hifi and radio hardware and a wide range of CDs.

● KESSEL'S ESPRESSO STUDIO
Friedrichstrasse 54 (City Centre)
▲ Bertha-von-Suttner-Platz/Beethoven-Haus
◆ Mon-Fri 10am-7pm, Sat 10am-6pm
www.kessels-espresso-studio.de

Whether you need an espresso machine or just the accessories, you will find what you want here.

● PAPIER & BUCH

Bonner Talweg 46 (Südstadt)
▲ Weberstrasse
◆ Mon-Fri 8am-7pm,
Sat 9am-2.30pm
www.papierundbuch-bonn.de

Whether it's a book or something else, here you will find lots of ideas for gifts.

● PUPPENKÖNIG

Gangolfstrasse 8-10
(City Centre)
▲ Universität/Markt
◆ Mon-Fri 9.30am-7pm,
Sat 9.30am-6pm
www.puppenkoenig.de

Paradise for children large and small for over 135 years.

● SHOP IM BEETHOVEN-HAUS

Bonngasse 18-26 (City Centre)
▲ Bertha-von-Suttner-Platz/Beethoven-Haus
◆ 10am-6.30pm (April-Oct), Mon-Sat 10am-6pm,
Sun 11am-5pm (Nov-March)
www.beethoven-haus-bonn.de

This shop sells all sorts of things connected with Beethoven and his home town.

● LUDUS SPIELWAREN

Friedrichstrasse 14-16
(City Centre)
▲ Bertha-von-Suttner-Platz/Beethoven-Haus
◆ Mon-Fri 10am-7pm,
Sat 10am-5pm
www.ludus-spielwaren.de

From wooden toys to cuddly toys, here you will find lovely things to play with and collect for all ages.

● WEINKOMMISSAR

Friedrichstrasse 20
(City Centre)
▲ Bertha-von-Suttner-Platz/Beethoven-Haus
◆ Mon-Fri 10am-11pm
www.weinkommissar.de

A tip for wine lovers: good German, Italian, Austrian and Slovenian wines can be sampled here.

GUMMY BEARS AND FRIENDS

A small backyard laundry in Kessenich, a district of Bonn, is the place where the success story of a well-known company began in 1920. The company name, Haribo, was taken from its founder and the place where it started: **Ha**ns **Ri**egel **Bo**nn. Two years later Riegel invented bears made from fruit gum, which were to become a world-famous cult product under the name Haribo Gold Bears. Since those days many new products have been added to the assortment, but the advertising slogan invented in 1935 still holds good: "Haribo macht Kinder froh – und Erwachsene ebenso" (Haribo makes children happy – adults too). The company has had an equally durable partnership with the TV presenter Thomas Gottschalk, who has advertised the bears for more than 20 years.

Factory outlet
Friesdorfer Strasse 21
(Bad Godesberg)
◆ *Mon-Fri 9.30am-6pm,*
Sat 9.30am-4pm
www.haribo.com

3 **TIP** On seven Saturdays a year, Bonn presents a special event for shoppers: 1800 traders from all over Germany come to the **flea market in the Rheinaue**. Everything is to be found, from kitsch and junk to antiques and clothes, so long as it is second-hand.
www.flohmarkt-rheinaue.de

Useful Addresses

THE "BONN BALL PAINTING"

... is proof that Bonn has been a stronghold of Rhenish Carnival even longer than its neighbour Cologne. Whereas the first evidence for celebrations in Cologne goes back to 1823, a work by the court painter François Rousseau dating from 1754 depicts a colourful mix of Carnival society, both aristocrats and the upper bourgeoisie. Masked balls took place twice weekly in winter, and every evening in the week of Carnival. They were so famous that even Casanova enthused about them on his visit in 1760. But Carnival in Bonn is even older than that, as shown by the police regulations that Prince Elector Ernst of Bavaria issued there in the late 16th century in an attempt to prevent the wildest excesses of the celebrations.

INFORMATION

● **BONN-INFORMATION**
Windeckstrasse 1
on Münsterplatz
Tel. 0228/775000
▲ Hauptbahnhof
◆ Mon-Fri 10am-6pm, Sat 10am-4pm, Sun 10am-2pm
www.bonn.de

ARRIVING/DEPARTING

● **COLOGNE-BONN AIRPORT**
Heinrich-Steinmann-Str. 12
51147 Köln
Tel. 02203/404001/02
www.koeln-bonn-airport.de

Cologne-Bonn Airport is 26 kilometres from the centre of Bonn.

BUS: the express bus SB60 takes only 25 minutes from the terminal to the main station in the city centre.

TAXI + SHUTTLESERVICE: At Terminals 1 and 2 there are cab ranks. Shuttle service:
www.koelnerflugshuttle.de,
Tel. 0221/29998118.

Car hire in Terminal 2, level 0:
Avis: 02203/402343
Europcar: 02203/955880
Hertz: 02203/402501
Sixt Autovermietung:
0180/6262525

● **HAUPTBAHNHOF BONN**
(main train station)
Am Hauptbahnhof 1
Tel. 0180/5996633
◆ 6am-midnight
www.bahn.de

All the main tram and bus lines leave from the main station.

Taxis can be found at the north, south and middle entrances.

HIRE CARS: Europcar in DB Reisezentrum,
Tel. 0228/60434440;
Hertz, Tel. 0228/201530
◆ Mon-Fri 7.30am-6pm, Sat 8am-12 noon

BIKE HIRE: Radstation, Quantiusstrasse 26
Tel. 0228/9814636
◆ Mon-Fri 6am-10.30pm, Sat 7am-10.30pm, Sun 8am-10.30pm
www.radstationbonn.de

BANKS

Banks in Bonn are open at the usual times (approx. 9am-4pm).

● **REISEBANK**
Bonn Hauptbahnhof
Arnulf-Klett-Platz 2
◆ Mon-Fri 9am-7pm, Sat 9am-3pm

BOX OFFICE

● **BONNTICKET**
Adenauerallee 131
(City Centre)
Tel. 0228/502010
www.bonnticket.de

● **MR. MUSIC**
Maximilianstrasse 24
(City Centre)
Tel. 0228/690901
www.mrmusic.com

● **THEATER- UND
KONZERTKASSE**
Windeckstrasse 1 (City
Centre)
Tel. 0228/778008
www.theater-bonn.de

● **KAMMERSPIELE
BOX OFFICE**
Am Michaelshof 9
(Bad Godesberg)
Tel. 0228/778022/33
www.theater-bonn.de

MEDIA

PRINT: General-Anzeiger,
Express, Kölner Stadt-
anzeiger, Kölnische Rund-
schau, Bonnaparte,
Schnüss

RADIO + TV: Deutsche
Welle, Phoenix, Bundes-
studio WDR, Radio Bonn/
Rhein-Sieg, bonncampus
96,8, Radio 96,8

EMERGENCY

Police: Tel. 110
Fire brigade: Tel. 112
Ambulance:
Tel. 19222 (from mobile
phone dial code 0228)
Emergency doctor:
Tel. 116117
Private emergency doctor:
Tel. 0228/19257
Emergency dentist:
Tel. 01805986700
Emergency pharmacy:
Tel. 01805002963
ADAC breakdown service:
Tel. 01802/222222
Lost and found:
Tel. 0228/772586

PUBLIC TRANSPORT

● **STADTWERKE BONN**
Verkehrs-GmbH
Sandkaule 2
53111 Bonn
Tel. 0228/7111
www.swb-busundbahn.de

SERVICE CENTRES:
Poststrasse 2
◆ Mon-Fri 6.30am-7pm,
Sat 9am-2pm

SWB-Verkaufsstelle,
Central Bus Station
◆ Mon-Fri 6.30am-7pm,
Sat 9am-2pm

Alte Bahnhofsstrasse
22a Bad Godesberg
◆ Mon-Fri 6.30am-7pm,
Sat 9am-2pm

GUIDED TOURS

● **BONN FÜHRUNGEN
KERKHOFF**
Tel. 0228/694712
*www.bonnfuehrungen-
kerkhoff.de*

● **BONNER STADT-
SPAZIERGANG WITH
RAINER SEELMANN M.A.**
Tel. 0228/697682
www.kultnews.de

● **GUIDE SERVICE
FROM BONN-INFOR-
MATION**
Tel. 0228/773921

● **STATTREISEN BONN
ERLEBEN E.V.**
Tel. 0228/654553
www.stattreisen-bonn.de

TAXI

● **TAXI BONN E.G.**
Tel. 0228/555555
www.taxibonn.de

● **TAXIBETRIEB
FARINAZ SHAKOUIE**
Tel. 0175 8308305,
0163-7427512
www.taxibonn.com

● **TAXI GAUCHEL**
Tel. 0173/2803040
www.taxigauchel.de

● **VV-TAXI**
Tel. 0228/282824
www.taxi-bonn.de

Bonn's History

12000 BC	A man and a woman with a dog are buried on the Stingenberg in Oberkassel.
4080 BC	There is a fortified settlement on the Venusberg.
30 BC	The Ubii tribe settle the area between the university and the minster.
13–9 BC	The Roman general Drusus establishes a reconnaissance camp in the Ubii settlement.
69	First written mention of the camp, as "castra Bonnensia" in Tacitus' *Histories*.
Approx. 450	After attacks by the Franks, the Romans abandon the camp, which is now called Bonnburg.
804	First written mention of the "villa basilica", a settlement near the minster, the heart of the medieval and present-day city.
1151	Consecration of the double church at Schwarzrheindorf.
1167	The collegiate church of St Cassius is granted the right to hold a three-day market free of dues.
1244	On the orders of Konrad von Hochstaden, archbishop of Cologne, the market town is surrounded by a wall.
1288	After the battle of Worringen, Bonn becomes a favoured place for the prince electors (archbishops of Cologne) to stay.
1597	Bonn is an official residence of the prince electors.
1697	Prince Elector Joseph Clemens starts to rebuild the palace.
1770	Ludwig van Beethoven is baptised in the church of St Remigius.

NEUEINGÄNGE
für den
Herrn Bundeskanzler

1786 Prince Elector Maximilian Franz elevates the academy to the status of a university.

1794 French troops occupy the town.

1815 Following the Congress of Vienna, Bonn becomes part of Prussia.

1818 Refoundation of the Rheinische Friedrich-Wilhelms-Universität.

1845 The first Beethovenfest is held.

1898 Construction of the first bridge between Bonn and Beuel.

1944 An air raid destroys almost the whole city centre.

1949 Bonn becomes provisional federal capital.

1969 Incorporation of Bad Godesberg and Beuel into Bonn.

1989 Bonn celebrates its 2000th birthday.

1990 Berlin is named capital of Germany in the treaty on German unification.

1992 Opening of the Kunstmuseum.

1994 The Berlin/Bonn Law regulates the division of work between the two cities.

1996 Bonn becomes a UN city.

2000 Construction of the Post-Tower begins

2006 The UN-Campus is opened.

2015 The World Conference Center Bonn is completed.

Picture Credits
All photos BKB Verlag except Ameron Hotel Königshof Bonn 50 ab., Arp Museum Bahnhof Rolandseck/ Laura Padgett 43 ab., Beethoven-Fest/Barbara Frommann 7, 14 be., 60-61 ab., Beethoven-Fest/ Danetzki & Weidner, Kornelia Danetzki 22 ab., Beethoven-Halle/Frank Fremerey 15 Mi.r., Beethoven-Haus 14 ab.r., 15 Mi.l., U1 be.l., Beethoven-Haus /Sonja Wener 15 ab.l., Bonner Münster 10 Mi., 11 Mr., 12 ab., 13 ab., Derag Livinghotel Kanzler 59 be., Deutsche Post AG 31 Mi.r., Frauenmuseum 65 Mi.l., Haus der Springmaus e.V. 62 u, Juba Wellness Tempel 58 Mi., Junges Theater Bonn 61 be., 63 be., Kunst- und Ausstellungshalle/ Peter Oszvald 47 ab.l., be., Kunst- und Ausstellungshalle/Tania Beifuß 47 ab.r., Kunstmuseum Bonn 48 ab., LVR-Museumsverbund/Hans-Theo Gerhards 64 be.l., Pantheon Theater GmbH 21, 63 ab., Presseamt der Bundesstadt Bonn 30 Mi., Presseamt der Bundesstadt Bonn/Michael Sondermann U1 be.r., U8, 2-3, 16 ab., 17 ab., 19 ab., 20 be.r., 22 be., 24 ab., 31 ab., 32 be., 35 ab., be.r., 38 Mi., 39, 40 be.l., 41 Mi., 45, 47 ab.Mi., 55 be.r., 56 Mi., 57 Mi., 64-65 Mi., 65 ab., Mi.r., 66 Mi., Schlösser Augustusburg und Falkenlust/Florian Monheim 36 Mi., Theater im Ballsaal 62 ab., Tourismus & Congress GmbH Region Bonn/Rhein-Sieg/Ahrweiler 6, 19 ab., 50 be., 55 be., Universität Bonn/Frank Luerweg 64 ab., Universität Bonn/Frank Homann 20 ab.l., World Conference Center Bonn 51 Mi.